GOTHAM CENTRAL

HALF A LIFE

GREG RUCKA WRITER

MICHAEL LARK ARTIST, "HALF A LIFE"

JASON PEARSON & CAM SMITH
ARTISTS, "TWO DOWN"

WILLIAM ROSADO & STEVE MITCHELL
ARTISTS, "HAPPY BIRTHDAY TWO YOU..."

MATT HOLLINGSWORTH
DIGITAL CHAMELEON
WILDSTORM FX

COLORISTS

WILLIE SCHUBERT
RICK PARKER
TODD KLEIN

LETTERERS

BATMAN CREATED BY **BOB KANE**

Dan DiDio VP-EXECUTIVE EDITOR • Matt Idelson, Dennis O'Neil, Jordan Gorfinkel EDITORS-ORIGINAL SERIES
Nachie Castro ASSISTANT EDITOR-ORIGINAL SERIES • Robert Greenberger SENIOR EDITOR-COLLECTED EDITION
Robbin Brosterman SENIOR ART DIRECTOR • Amie Brockway-Metcalf ART DIRECTOR • Paul Levitz PRESIDENT & PUBLISHER
Georg Brewer VP-DESIGN & RETAIL PRODUCT DEVELOPMENT • Richard Bruning SR. VP-CREATIVE DIRECTOR
Patrick Caldon SR. VP-FINANCE & OPERATIONS • Chris Caramalis VP-FINANCE • Terri Cunningham VP-MANAGING EDITOR
Stephanie Fierman SR. VP-SALES & MARKETING • Alison Gill VP-MANUFACTURING • Rich Johnson VP-BOOK TRADE SALES
Hank Kanalz VP-GENERAL MANAGER, WILDSTORM • Lillian Laserson SR. VP & GENERAL COUNSEL • Jim Lee EDITORIAL
DIRECTOR-WILDSTORM • Paula Lowitt SR. VP-BUSINESS & LEGAL AFFAIRS • David McKillips VP-ADVERTISING & CUSTOM
PUBLISHING • John Nee VP-BUSINESS DEVELOPMENT • Gregory Noveck SR. VP-CREATIVE AFFAIRS • Cheryl Rubin
SR. VP-BRAND MANAGEMENT • Bob Wayne VP-SALES

GOTHAM CENTRAL: HALF A LIFE.

INTRODUCTION

BY GREG RUCKA

Renee Montoya was the first person I met when I came to Gotham City. She wasn't a detective, yet, just a patrol officer, just one of a handful of honest cops in a department—hell, in a city—renowned for corruption and cruelty. She'd never heard of me. At that point, in fact, no one really had.

Except for then-Batman Group Editor Denny O'Neil, who was ultimately responsible for the introduction. It was entirely accidental. I knew him because, well, he was Denny O'Neil. He knew me through my novels. Through a mixture of right place, right time, and right people, Denny offered me a job, or, more specifically, a tryout. Write a story, he said, 22 pages, for BATMAN CHRONICLES, and we'll see where that takes us.

I asked him if I could write a Two-Face story, and Denny nodded sagely, because just about everyone, I suspect, writes a Two-Face story for their Batman tryout. Either that or a Joker story, but, truth be told, I've never much cared for Joker. Harvey Dent, Two-Face, on the other hand, is one of those rare villains who is more than just a madman. He, like Batman, is tragic, and I have always found his particular tragedy compelling. Here's a man, once a good, moral, honorable man, who is now so lost and so broken that he can no longer decide between right and wrong, to such an extent he must leave it to chance, to the flip of a coin.

That's the thing with Two-Face. He doesn't flip the coin to decide steak or salad, to decide knife or gun. He flips to decide Good or Evil. Do I kill the baby? Or do I save it from the burning building?

So I thought I'd write this 22-page Two-Face story, and that it would be about the coin. About the fact that it's theoretically possible to flip heads twenty, thirty, forty times in a row. And that the Law of Averages demands that, in return, you'll flip tails twenty, thirty, or forty times in return. What would happen, I wondered, if Two-Face kept flipping "good"?

But I needed someone to see it, someone to witness Two-Face as a good guy, and it couldn't be Batman, because Batman feeds Harvey's madness, demands a coin toss by his very presence. Batman would have to act when faced with Two-Face, because he just cannot take the chance that Harvey will hit tails and, using the above example, kill the baby. Couldn't be Batman.

And that's how I met Renee, and that's how the story "Two Down" started.

When it ended, though, I knew it was something else. Two-Face and Officer Montoya had a connection, now. He knew her. And maybe, just maybe, he was a little crushed out on this cop who refused to let her fear of him rule her. He respected her. And Montoya, she understood him differently, she understood the coin. She was one of the only people in the world—if not the only person—who could see past Two-Face and speak to Harvey Dent.

Harvey, for his part, knew it, too.

How could he not love her for that?

◾ ◾ ◾ ◾ ◾

No Man's Land happened, this massive, year-long event story that ran throughout 1999. Two-Face was a warlord, ruler of his own sector of Gotham's ruins. Montoya fought for law and order with James Gordon and what was left of the cops. And somewhere along the line, Two-Face decided he would "take care" of Montoya's family. He would protect them. It was, in his madness, the way he would demonstrate his affection for her.

Montoya, as you might imagine, didn't see it that way. Especially not when he kidnapped her, held her hostage.

And again, Renee reached out to Harvey, spoke to him through Two-Face's madness, and now both Harvey Dent and Two-Face were falling for her, and falling hard.

◾ ◾ ◾ ◾ ◾

Gotham was rebuilt, *No Man's Land* ended, and Renee Montoya was promoted to Detective,

given a position in the Major Crimes Unit. The MCU are Gotham's best detectives, best cops, all of them honest, all of them committed to their work. Hand-picked by the Commissioner to serve in the squad, they're tasked with investigating the worst of Gotham's crimes. They are the heart of GOTHAM CENTRAL.

So Montoya worked the MCU, and Two-Face went back to Arkham. And maybe she could forget about him, but he couldn't forget about her. He even remembered her birthday. He began to imagine that she might love him the way he loved her.

He forgot one thing:

Ordinary people have secret identities, too.

◾ ◾ ◾ ◾ ◾

All right, spoiler warning: if you haven't read "Half a Life" yet, skip this bit until you finish the story. Honestly. It's not a huge thing, but it's part of the drama, and neither Michael Lark nor I would want to spoil it for you in advance (and here's hoping the cover copy didn't already give it away).

Seriously. I'll wait.

◾ ◾ ◾ ◾ ◾

People got angry at this story. They accused me and Michael Lark of all sorts of things, almost all of them without basis in fact, and almost all of them revealing far more about the accusers than the accused. It's always seemed ridiculous to me that there was such a tempest in a teapot. Most ridiculous to me was the accusation that we "made" Montoya gay.

As far as I'm concerned, we did no such thing. She was always gay. We were simply the first story to actually say so, and to say it in no uncertain terms. We were, I'm told, the first comic book story in the DCU to actually have a character say the words, "I'm a lesbian."

Tempest in a teapot.

Comics are art, and they are literature, and, yes, they are entertainment. None of those things must exclude the others. For any story to be successful, it must reflect the truths of our own world, the things we all share—love and loss and pain and fear and even the smaller things, the frustration of losing our car keys, the joy at finding a forgotten twenty in a coat pocket. As in our own world, comics cannot be solely stories of straight white Christian males.

Some people don't like to be reminded of that, I suspect. Some people don't like to be challenged. Some people think comics are for kids, and that kids are either naïve, stupid, or incapable of making up their own minds. I'm not one of those people. Neither is Michael Lark, and, thankfully, neither is the editorial staff at DC Comics.

I remember talking to Michael on the phone, just before we began working on "Half a Life." I remember telling him that this was the story I'd been waiting to tell ever since I'd finished "Two Down," that from the moment I'd finished that one, I'd known I would write this one. From the start, this was where I was heading with Montoya and Two-Face.

At this point in my career, I've written some dozen novels, and God only knows how many comics. Michael Lark, for his part, has turned out hundreds if not thousands of pages of stunning graphic storytelling.

I can safely speak for us both when I say that "Half a Life" is the story of which we are the proudest. It's a good story.

It is, dare I say it, a damn good story.

We hope you'll think so, too.

GREG RUCKA

Portland, Oregon
January, 2005

AFTER THE CATACLYSM, BEFORE NO MAN'S LAND...

ALL-RISK INSURANCE!! CALL NOW!

"I'M SO TIRED...

"...I DON'T THINK I'VE *EVER* BEEN THIS TIRED."

G.C.P.D. GOTHAM CITY POLICE DEPT.

--FORTY-EIGHT OFF. RECHARGE. *REST.* YOU'VE BEEN NONSTOP SINCE THE INITIAL QUAKE, AND YOU'RE ALMOST DEAD ON YOUR FEET...

I'M FINE, SIR--

--NOT *LISTENING,* DETECTIVE. IF I HAVE TO, I'LL *SUSPEND* YOU. NOW GET OUT OF HERE. THAT'S AN ORDER.

AND IF I SEE YOU BEFORE YOU'RE DONE WITH YOUR TWO DOWN, I'LL HAVE THE NATIONAL GUARD SHOOT YOU.

...YES, SIR.

...TAKE IT SO BAD. COMMISH SAID THE SAME THING TO ME.

SO, WHERE YOU GONNA GO, PARD?

DUNNO...

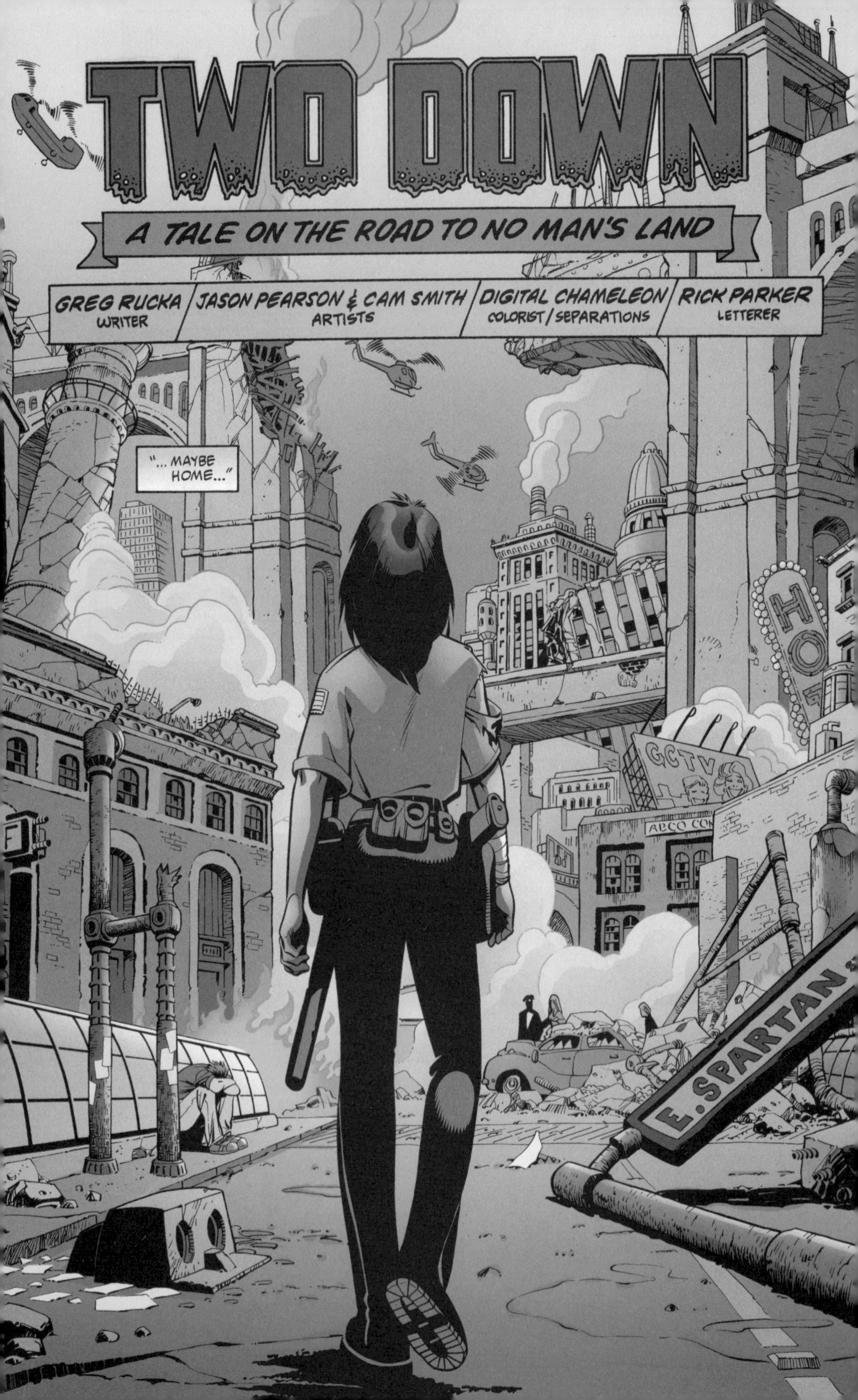
TWO DOWN
A TALE ON THE ROAD TO NO MAN'S LAND
GREG RUCKA WRITER
JASON PEARSON & CAM SMITH ARTISTS
DIGITAL CHAMELEON COLORIST / SEPARATIONS
RICK PARKER LETTERER
"... MAYBE HOME..."
GCTV
ABCO CO
E. SPARTAN

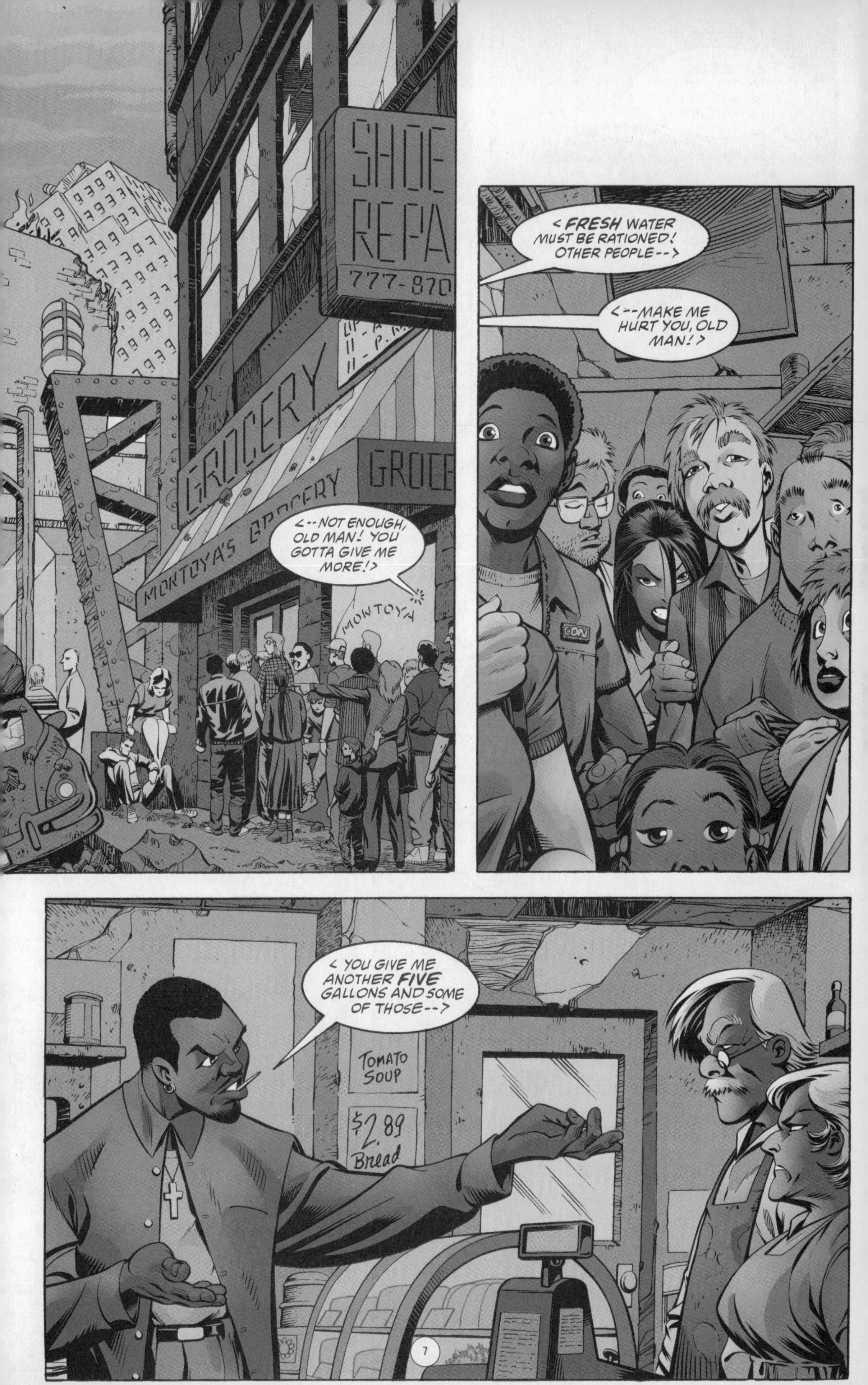
SHOE
REPA
777-870
GROCERY
MONTOYA'S GROCERY
GROC
MONTOYA
<--NOT ENOUGH, OLD MAN! YOU GOTTA GIVE ME MORE!>
<FRESH WATER MUST BE RATIONED! OTHER PEOPLE-->
<--MAKE ME HURT YOU, OLD MAN!>
<YOU GIVE ME ANOTHER FIVE GALLONS AND SOME OF THOSE-->
TOMATO SOUP
$2.89
Bread

< MIGUELITO... ≥TSK-TSK≤ STILL DON'T KNOW HOW TO SHARE, HUH?>

K-KICK

< TAKE YOUR RATION AND GET OUT OF MY PARENTS' STORE!>

CLAP CLAP CLAP CLAP CLAP

< IT'S EMPTY, ANYWAY. I RAN OUT OF BULLETS TWO DAYS AGO.>

<...WAVING THAT GUN AROUND LIKE THAT!>

< WORKED, THOUGH, DIDN'T IT, POPPA?>

< OUR DAUGHTER, SHE SHOULD PLAY POKER FOR A LIVING. >

< BETTER THAN BEING IN THE POLICE. COPS HAVEN'T EVEN BOTHERED WITH THIS PART OF TOWN SINCE THE EARTHQUAKE!>

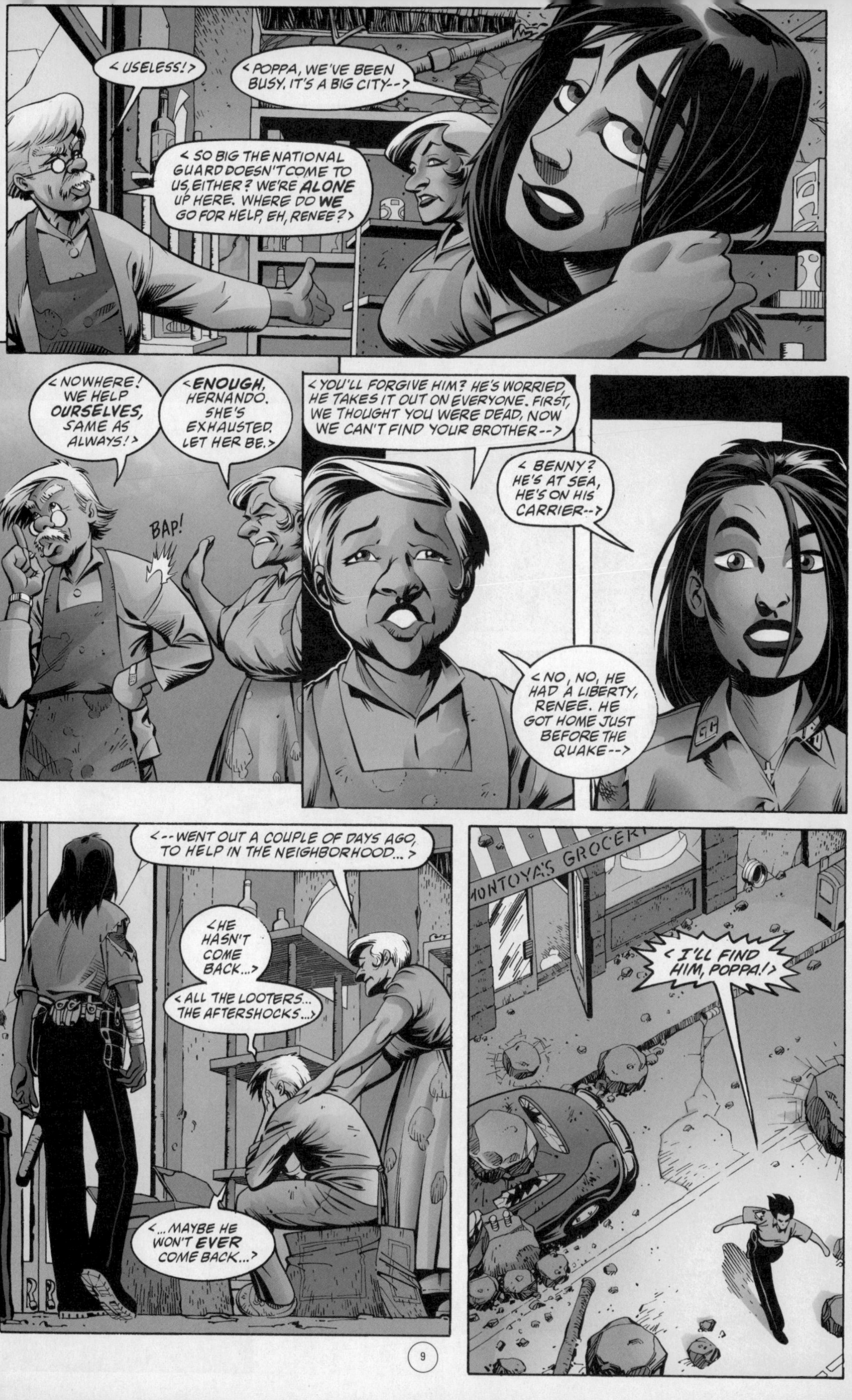
< USELESS! >
< POPPA, WE'VE BEEN BUSY. IT'S A BIG CITY-- >
< SO BIG THE NATIONAL GUARD DOESN'T COME TO US, EITHER? WE'RE ALONE UP HERE. WHERE DO WE GO FOR HELP, EH, RENEE? >
< NOWHERE! WE HELP OURSELVES, SAME AS ALWAYS! >
< ENOUGH, HERNANDO. SHE'S EXHAUSTED. LET HER BE. >
BAP!
< YOU'LL FORGIVE HIM? HE'S WORRIED, HE TAKES IT OUT ON EVERYONE. FIRST, WE THOUGHT YOU WERE DEAD, NOW WE CAN'T FIND YOUR BROTHER-- >
< BENNY? HE'S AT SEA, HE'S ON HIS CARRIER-- >
< NO, NO, HE HAD A LIBERTY, RENEE. HE GOT HOME JUST BEFORE THE QUAKE-- >
< --WENT OUT A COUPLE OF DAYS AGO, TO HELP IN THE NEIGHBORHOOD... >
< HE HASN'T COME BACK... >
< ALL THE LOOTERS... THE AFTERSHOCKS... >
< ...MAYBE HE WON'T EVER COME BACK... >
MONTOYA'S GROCER
< I'LL FIND HIM, POPPA! >

"THAT'S EASIER SAID THAN DONE...

"AND HERE I AM, SUPPOSED TO BE GETTING SOME...

"...REST.

"THEY'RE UP TO NO GOOD... MAYBE LOOTERS?

-- STILL UNDER THERE, AND WE'RE GOING TO GET THEM OUT! RIGHT?

RIGHT WITH YOU, HERMANO.

GET THAT SHOVEL OVER HERE. COME ON! MOVE!

"SOUNDS LIKE BENNY--

LET'S START DIGGING!

"-- BUT THAT OTHER GUY... I KNOW THAT VOICE..."

FREEZE! POLICE!!!

HANDS WHERE I CAN SEE THEM!

RELAX, OFFICER...

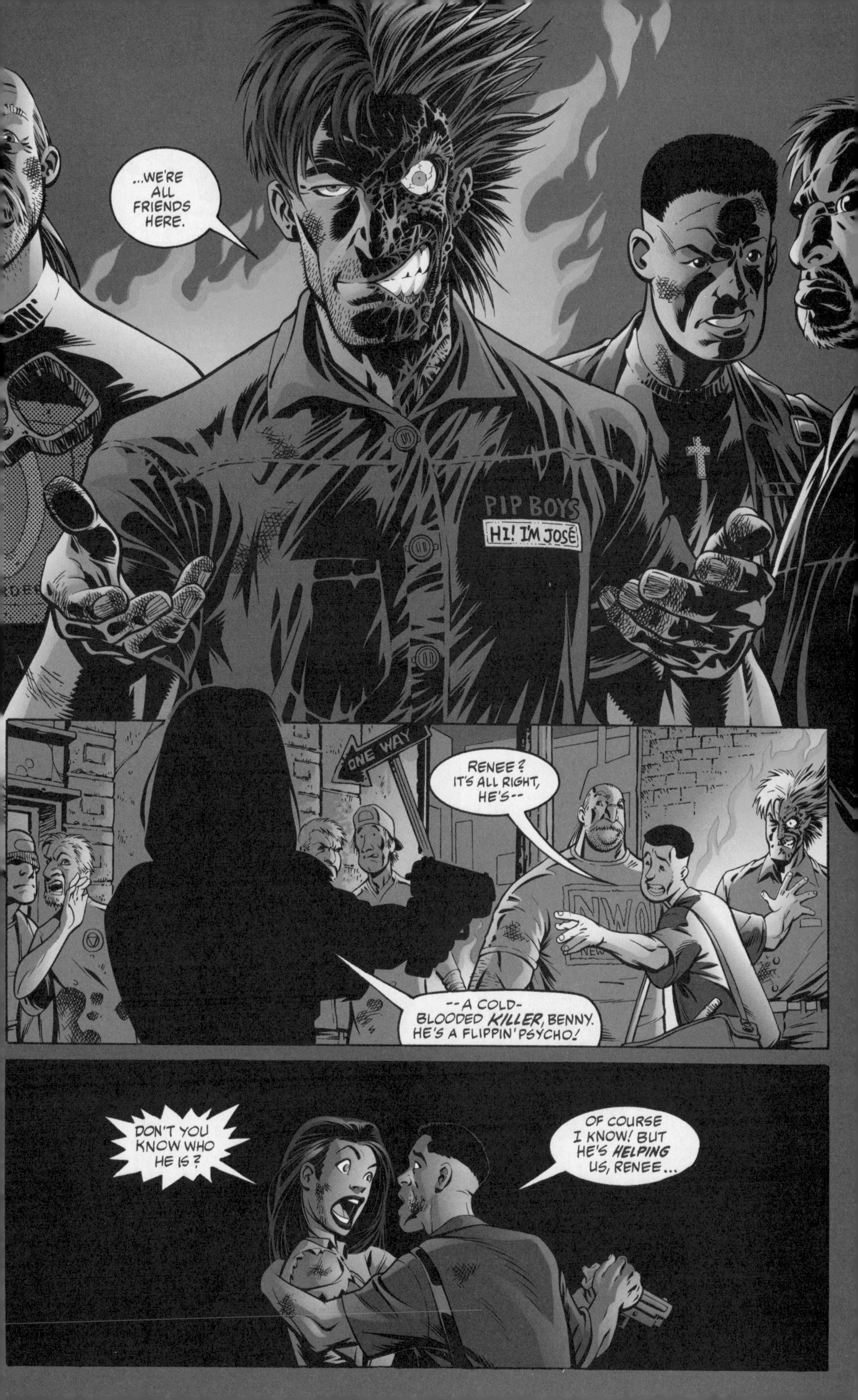
...WE'RE ALL FRIENDS HERE.
PIP BOYS
HI! I'M JOSÉ
ONE WAY
RENEE? IT'S ALL RIGHT, HE'S--
--A COLD-BLOODED KILLER, BENNY. HE'S A FLIPPIN' PSYCHO!
DON'T YOU KNOW WHO HE IS?
OF COURSE I KNOW! BUT HE'S HELPING US, RENEE...

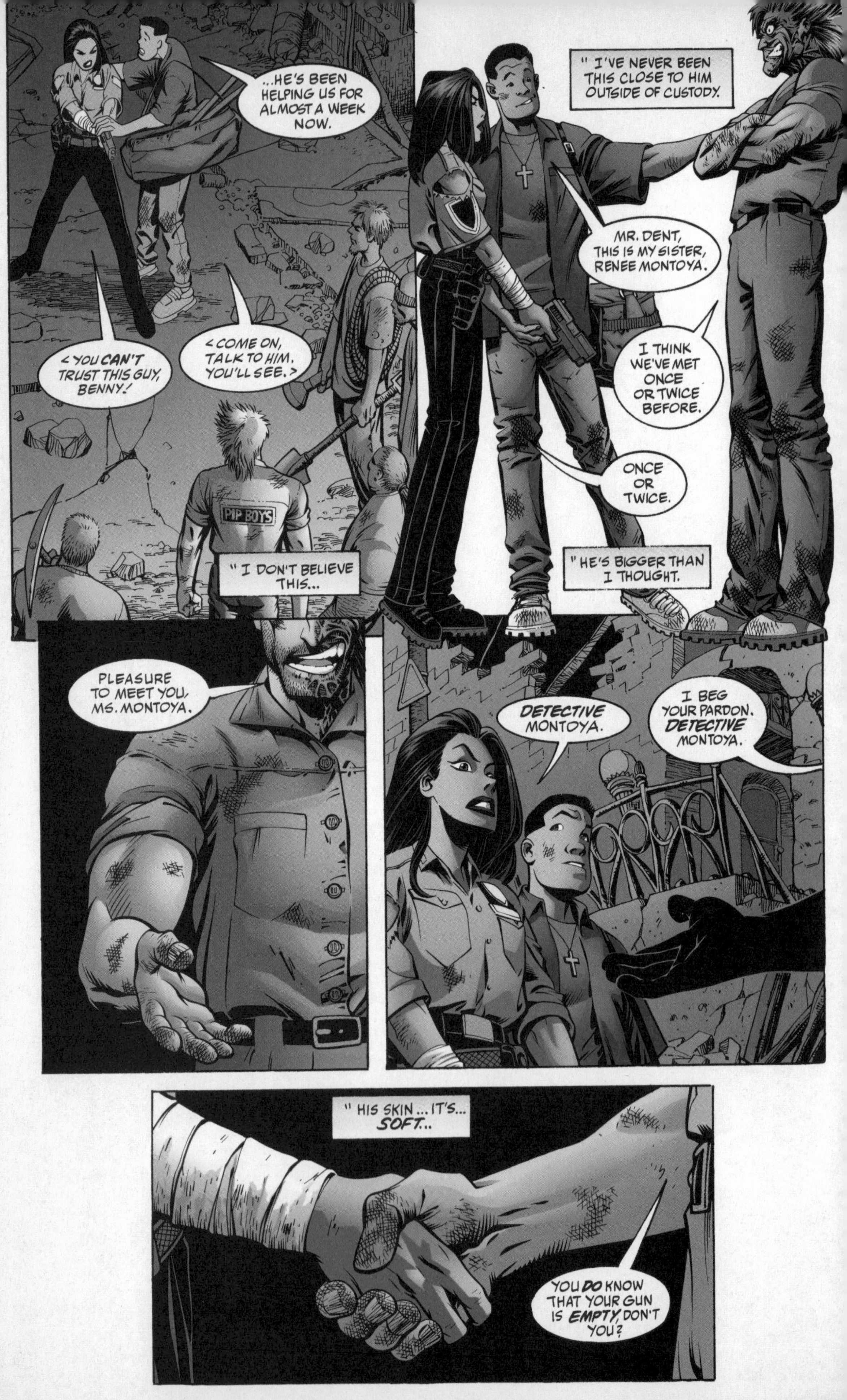

...HE'S BEEN HELPING US FOR ALMOST A WEEK NOW.
< YOU CAN'T TRUST THIS GUY, BENNY! >
< COME ON, TALK TO HIM. YOU'LL SEE. >
PIP BOYS
" I DON'T BELIEVE THIS...
" I'VE NEVER BEEN THIS CLOSE TO HIM OUTSIDE OF CUSTODY.
MR. DENT, THIS IS MY SISTER, RENEE MONTOYA.
I THINK WE'VE MET ONCE OR TWICE BEFORE.
ONCE OR TWICE.
" HE'S BIGGER THAN I THOUGHT.
PLEASURE TO MEET YOU, MS. MONTOYA.
DETECTIVE MONTOYA.
I BEG YOUR PARDON. DETECTIVE MONTOYA.
" HIS SKIN... IT'S... SOFT...
YOU DO KNOW THAT YOUR GUN IS EMPTY, DON'T YOU?

"I KEEP MY EYES ON HIM THE WHOLE TIME, EMPTY GUN OR NO."

GOT IT!

"HE'S A MONSTER AND HE'S CRAZY..."

ANYONE DOWN THERE?

"...IT'S JUST A MATTER OF TIME."

<...MISTER...?>

<MISTER?! DON'T LEAVE ME!>

<DON'T WORRY, SON. NO ONE'S LEAVING YOU.>

"DAWN, AND I *STILL* DON'T KNOW WHAT TO MAKE OF HIM.

...ALMOST CAN *REACH*...

" AND I'M NOT THE ONLY ONE.

<*THANK YOU!* OH, *THANK* YOU, *GOD* BLESS YOU! ...>

" I'M TOO *TIRED,* NOW...

COULD BE OTHERS IN THERE. WE SHOULD LOOK.

IT'S SAFER IF WE WORK IN GROUPS OF TWO. ONE PERSON CAN WATCH OUT FOR THE OTHER.

DETECTIVE?

" OR ELSE I NEVER WOULD'VE AGREED TO IT..."

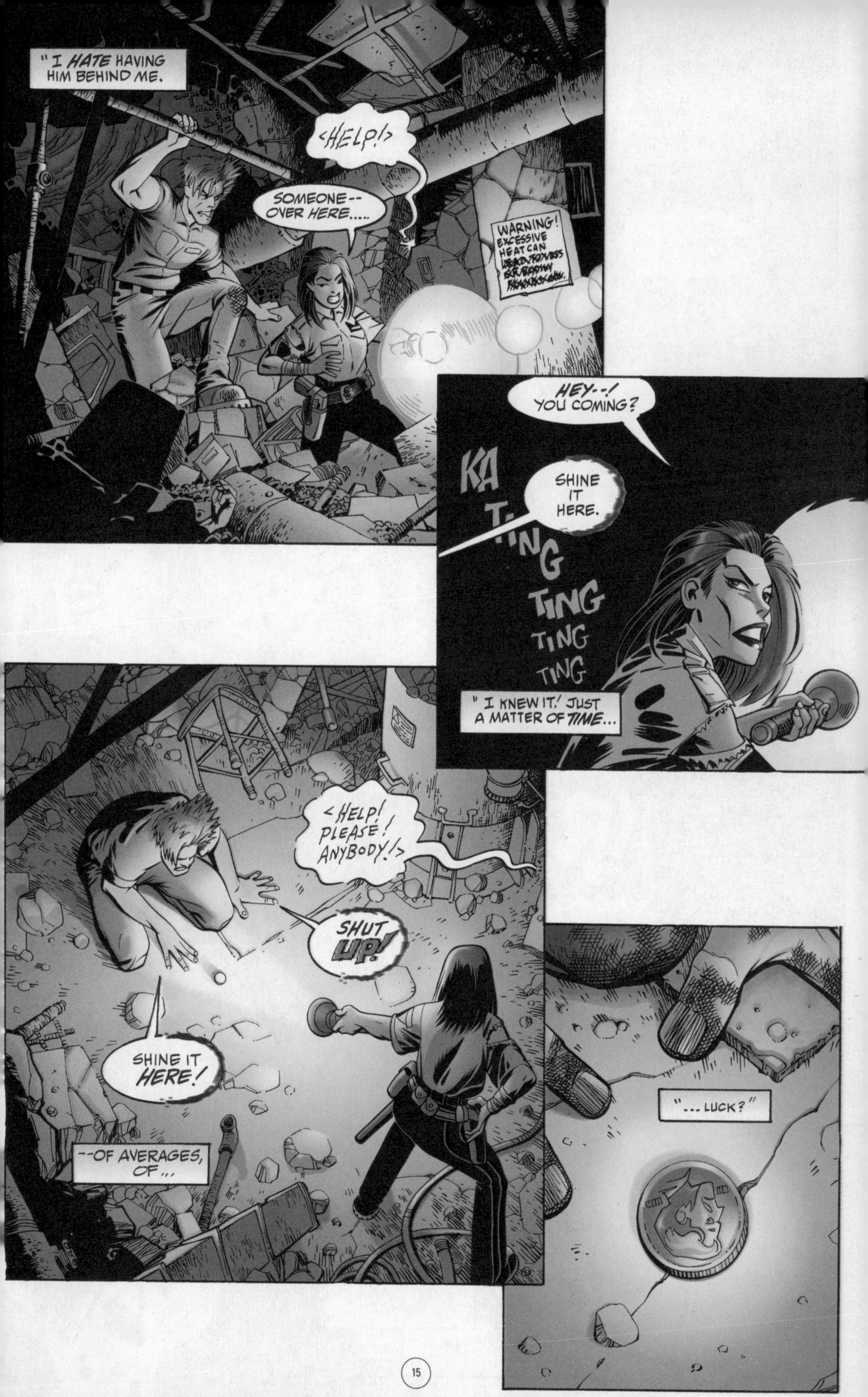

"I *HATE* HAVING HIM BEHIND ME.
<HELP!>
SOMEONE-- OVER *HERE*.....
WARNING! EXCESSIVE HEAT CAN
HEY--! YOU COMING?
KA TING
SHINE IT HERE.
TING
TING
TING
"I KNEW IT! JUST A MATTER OF *TIME*...
<HELP! PLEASE! ANYBODY!>
SHUT UP!
SHINE IT *HERE!*
--OF AVERAGES, OF...
"...LUCK?"

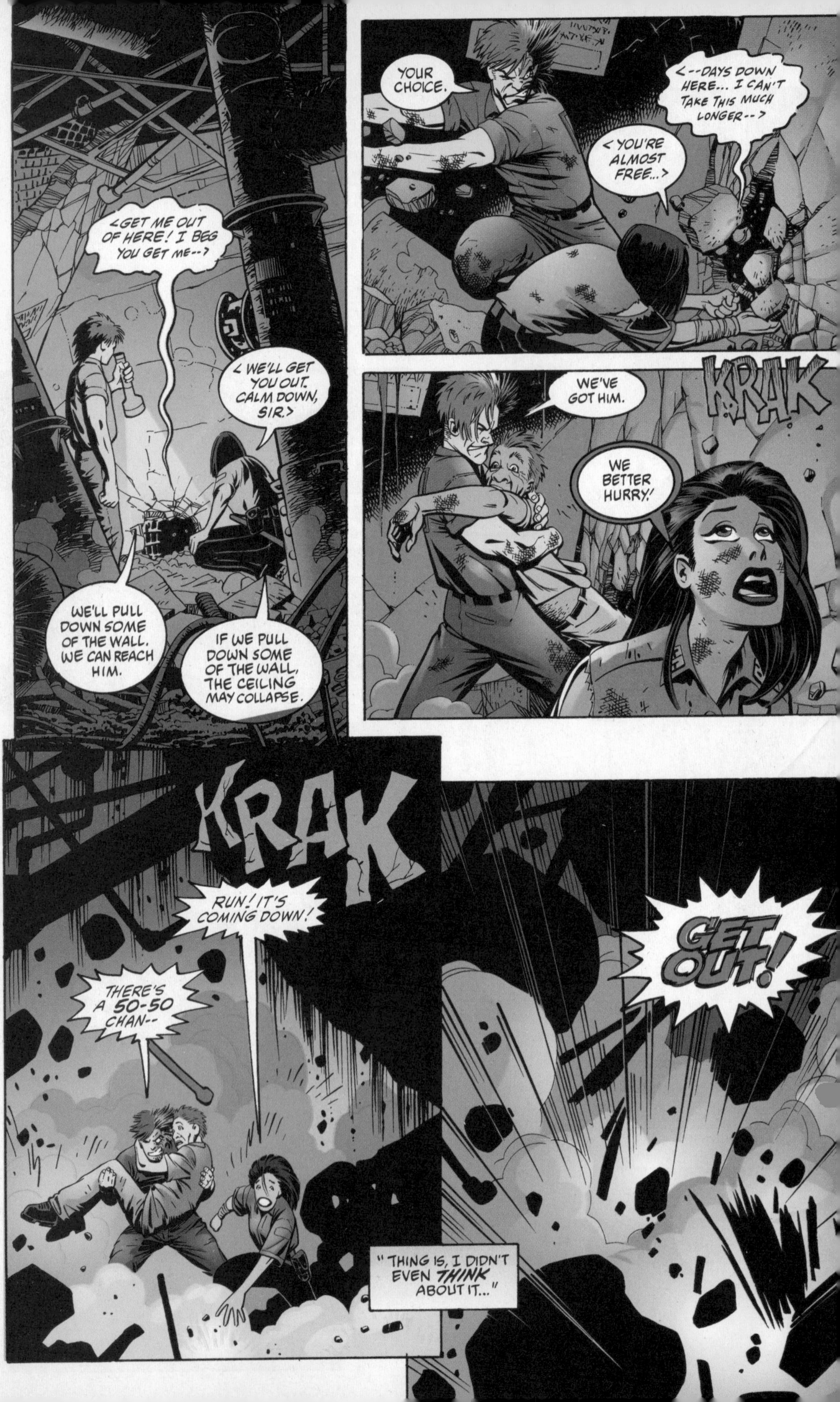
<GET ME OUT OF HERE! I BEG YOU GET ME-->
<WE'LL GET YOU OUT. CALM DOWN, SIR.>
WE'LL PULL DOWN SOME OF THE WALL. WE CAN REACH HIM.
IF WE PULL DOWN SOME OF THE WALL, THE CEILING MAY COLLAPSE.
YOUR CHOICE.
<--DAYS DOWN HERE... I CAN'T TAKE THIS MUCH LONGER-->
<YOU'RE ALMOST FREE...>
KRAK
WE'VE GOT HIM.
WE BETTER HURRY!
KRAK
RUN! IT'S COMING DOWN!
THERE'S A 50-50 CHAN--
GET OUT!
"THING IS, I DIDN'T EVEN THINK ABOUT IT..."

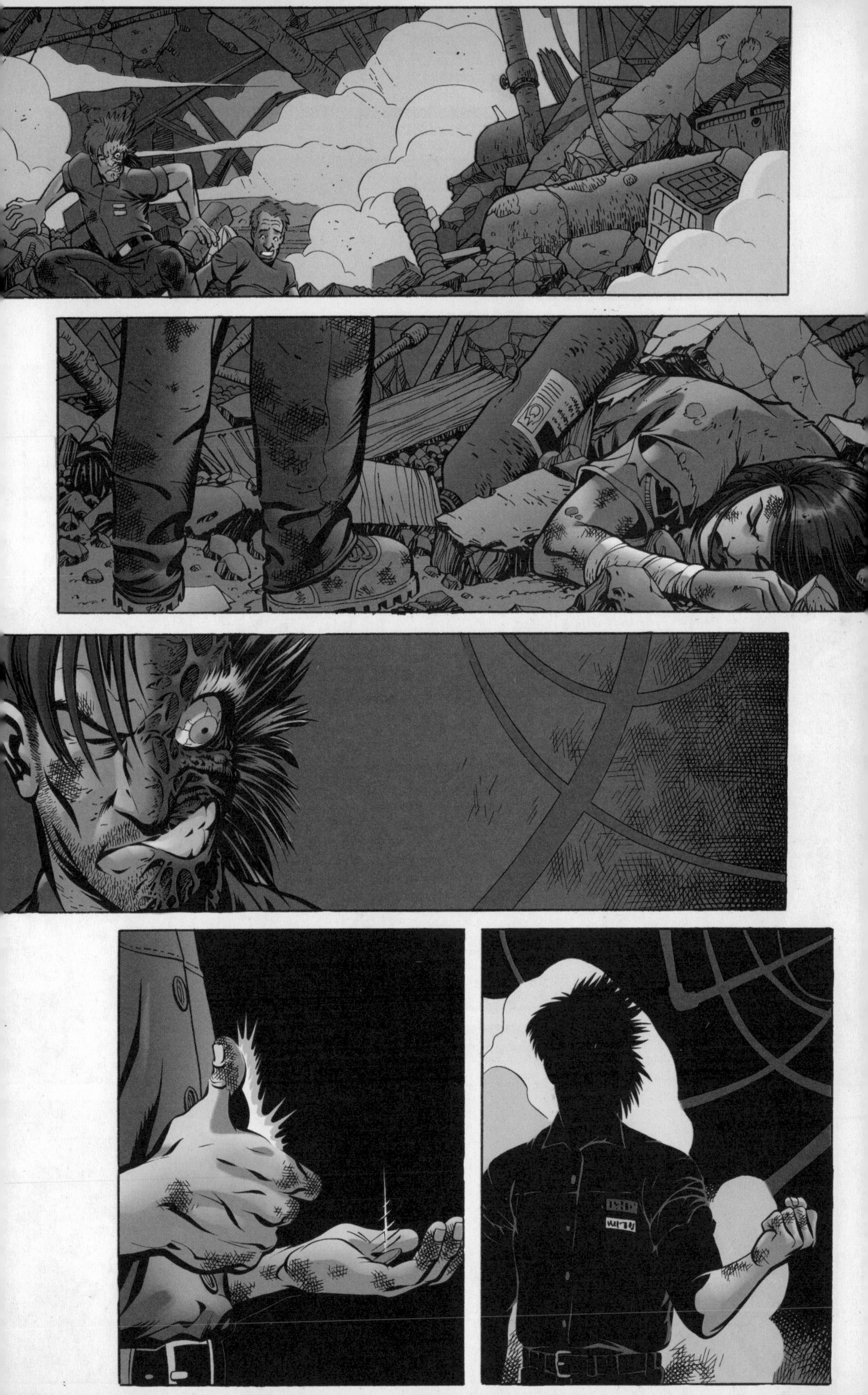

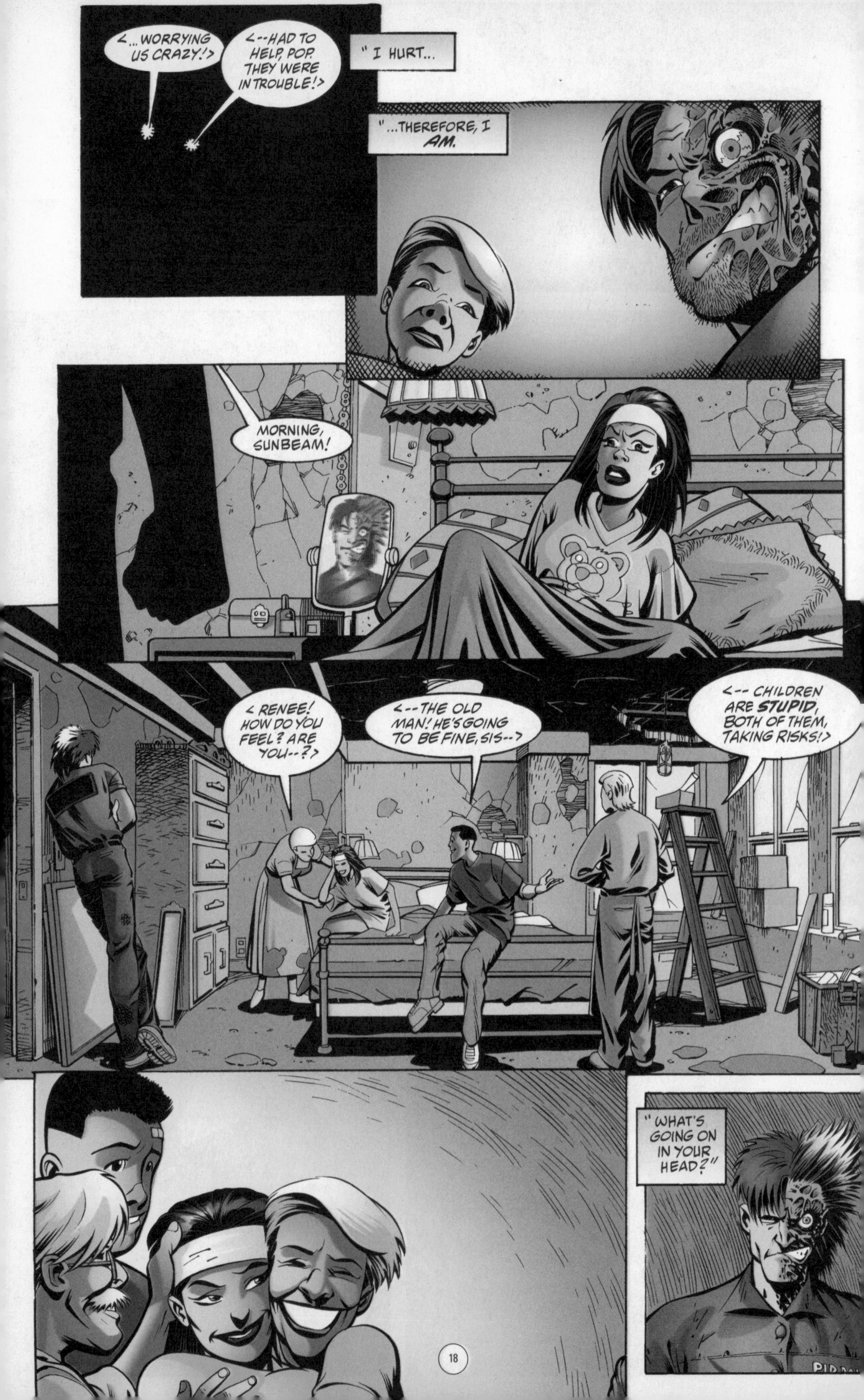
<...WORRYING US CRAZY!>
<--HAD TO HELP, POP. THEY WERE IN TROUBLE!>
"I HURT...
"...THEREFORE, I AM.
MORNING, SUNBEAM!
< RENEE! HOW DO YOU FEEL? ARE YOU--?>
<--THE OLD MAN! HE'S GOING TO BE FINE, SIS-->
<-- CHILDREN ARE STUPID, BOTH OF THEM, TAKING RISKS!>
"WHAT'S GOING ON IN YOUR HEAD?"

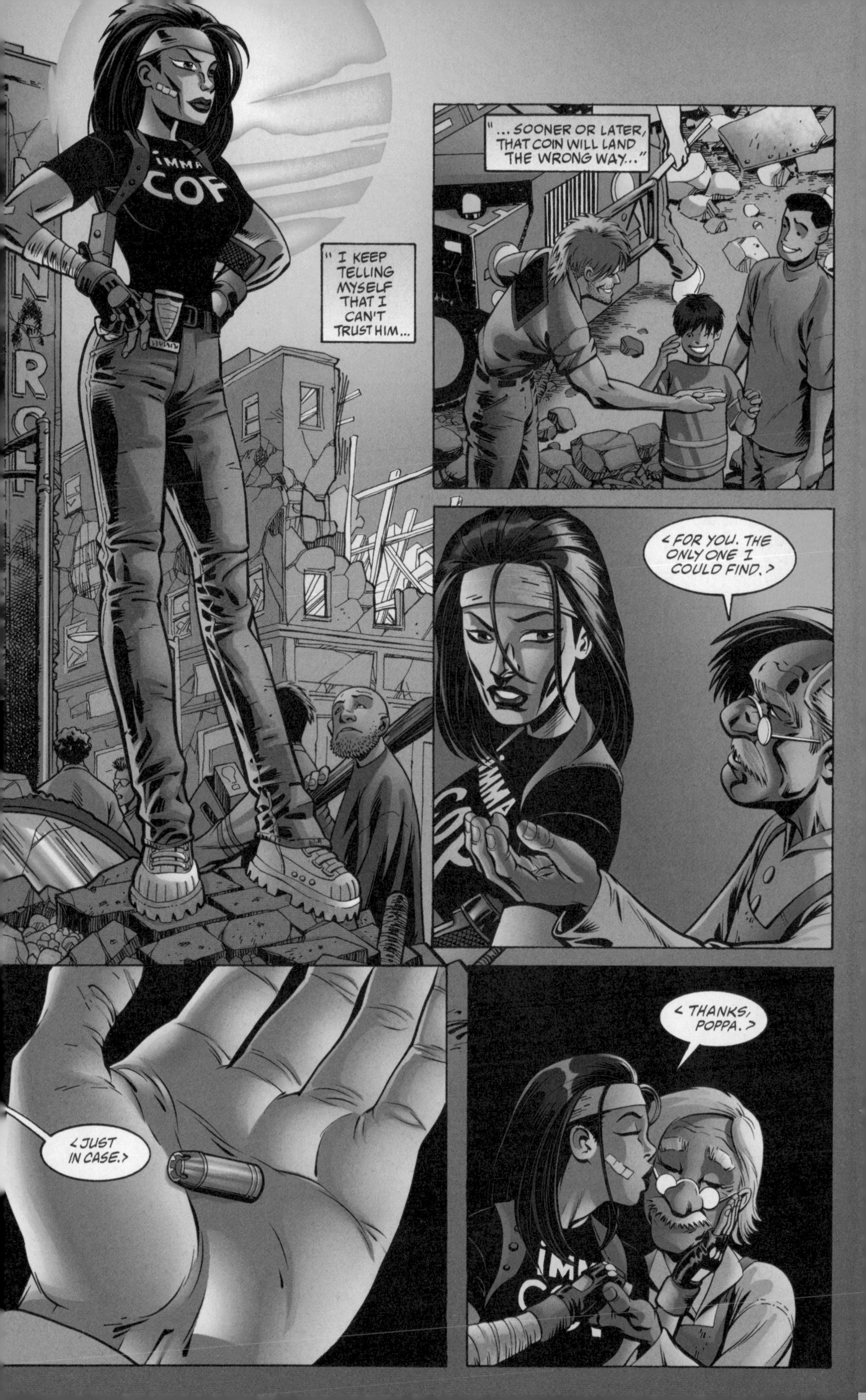
"I KEEP TELLING MYSELF THAT I CAN'T TRUST HIM...
"...SOONER OR LATER, THAT COIN WILL LAND THE WRONG WAY..."
<FOR YOU. THE ONLY ONE I COULD FIND.>
<JUST IN CASE.>
<THANKS, POPPA.>

" WE'RE AT IT ALL NIGHT.

"THE LAW OF AVERAGES DEMANDS THAT OUR LUCK WILL SOON RUN OUT. IT WON'T LAST. IT *CAN'T.*

"THREE TIMES HE FLIPS THAT COIN.

PIP BOYS

HI! I'M JOSÉ

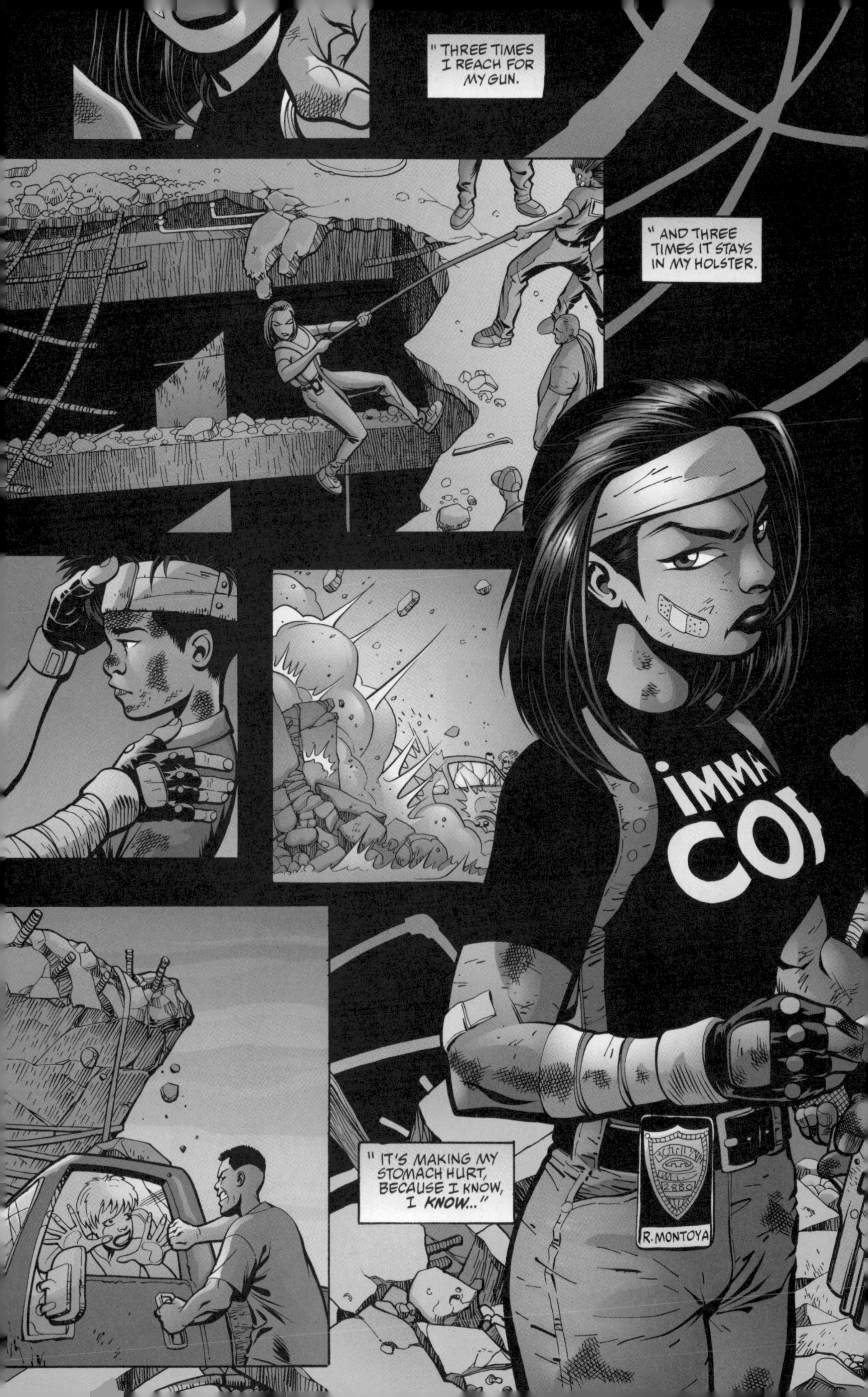
"THREE TIMES I REACH FOR MY GUN.
"AND THREE TIMES IT STAYS IN MY HOLSTER.
IMMA
CO
"IT'S MAKING MY STOMACH HURT, BECAUSE I KNOW, I *KNOW*..."
2880
R. MONTOYA

"... SOMETHING'S GOING TO HAPPEN...

"... AND IT'LL ALL END...

THERE'S NOTHING FOR YOU HERE. LEAVE.

TWO-FACE?

ASK HIM TO JOIN, ASK HIM, MICK!

YOU DON'T REMEMBER ME? WE WAS ON THAT BOAT TO BLACKGATE THAT ONE TIME! MICK WHITE! REMEMBER?

I...REMEMBER...

WHYN'T YOU JOIN US, MAN! WE COULD GET SOME REAL MONEY!

WHAT SAY WE TAKE A CHANCE?

" IT'S NOT CHANCE! IT'S NOT LUCK! IT'S JUST--

"-- AVERAGES!

WADDYA SAY, HUH?

I SAY--

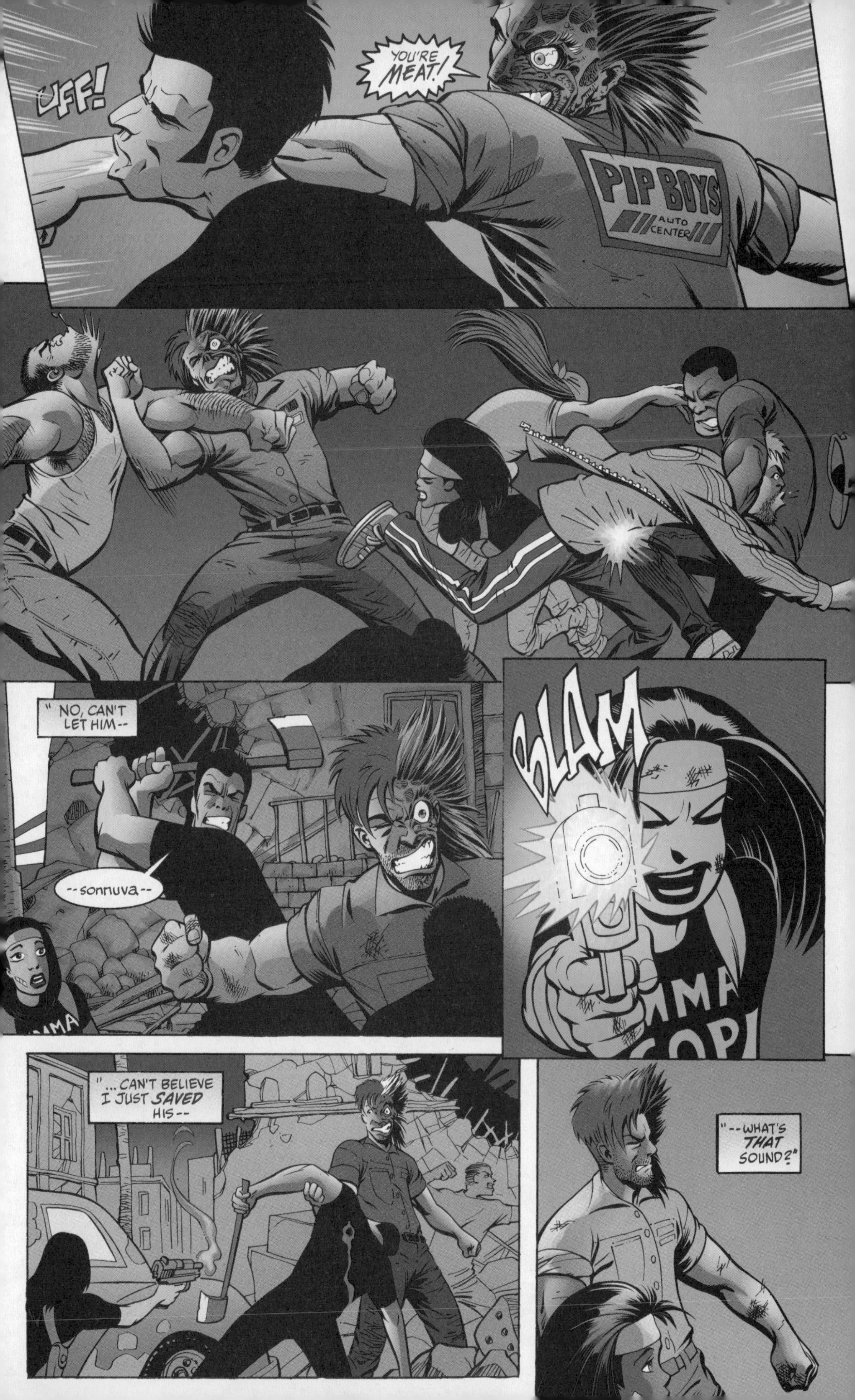
UFF!
YOU'RE MEAT!
PIP BOYS AUTO CENTER
" NO, CAN'T LET HIM--
--sonnuva--
BLAM
MMA COP
"...CAN'T BELIEVE I JUST SAVED HIS--
"--WHAT'S THAT SOUND?"

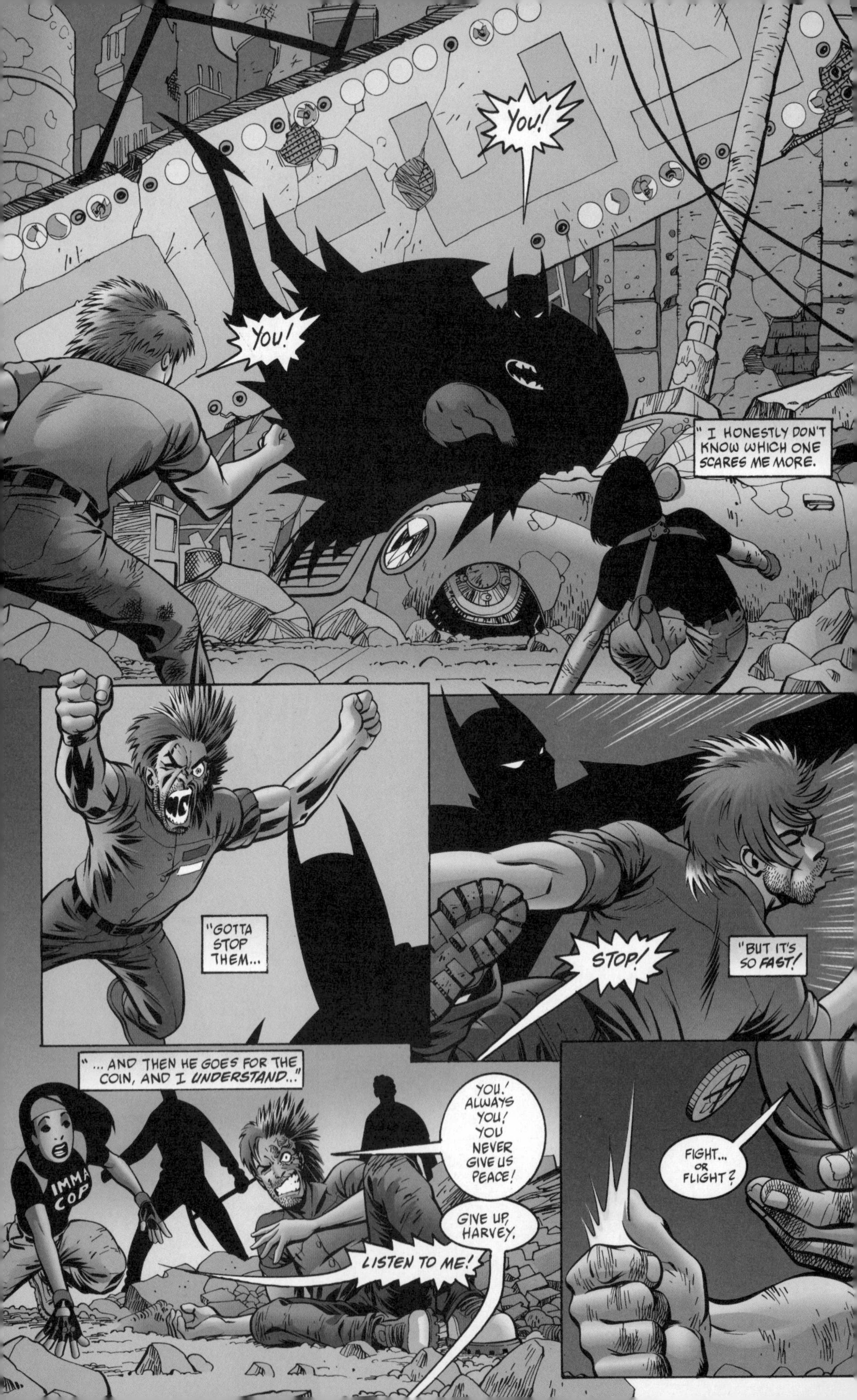

YOU!
YOU!
"I HONESTLY DON'T KNOW WHICH ONE SCARES ME MORE.
"GOTTA STOP THEM...
STOP!
"BUT IT'S SO FAST!
"...AND THEN HE GOES FOR THE COIN, AND I UNDERSTAND..."
YOU! ALWAYS YOU! YOU NEVER GIVE US PEACE!
GIVE UP, HARVEY.
LISTEN TO ME!
IMMA COP
FIGHT... OR FLIGHT?

NO!

"...AVERAGES, LUCK, CHANCE...

"...IT'S IRRELEVANT, IT DOESN'T MATTER.

WHAT DID IT SAY...? WHAT DID IT SAY? TELL US!

"THE COIN IS THE MOMENT, THAT'S ALL IT IS.

...DOUBLE-CROSSED...

NICELY DONE, DETECTIVE.

...PLEASE, TELL US...

LET HIM GO.

"AND THE MOMENT DOESN'T HAVE TO CHANGE.

"NOT YET, AT ANY RATE."

PLEASE. TRUST ME, JUST BACK OFF. IT'LL BE ALL RIGHT.

YOU REALIZE WHAT YOU'RE ASKING?

I HAVE TO TRY. PLEASE, BATMAN.

...I CAN REACH HIM...

THEN TRY, DETECTIVE.

I'LL WATCH.

... OUR COIN, RENEE, WE NEED TO KNOW...

LISTEN TO ME. IT DOESN'T MATTER, YOU HEAR? IT DOESN'T MATTER.

WE NEED TO KNOW...

NO, YOU *DON'T*... YOU *ALREADY* KNEW.

YOU WERE HELPING US! THAT DOESN'T HAVE TO CHANGE.

IT DOESN'T?

YOU JUST NEED TO FINISH WHAT YOU STARTED, THAT'S ALL. HE'S JUST AN INTERRUPTION-- *NOT* A CHOICE.

I'LL KEEP THE COIN FOR NOW. JUST UNTIL WE FINISH.

OKAY.

NOT THE END...

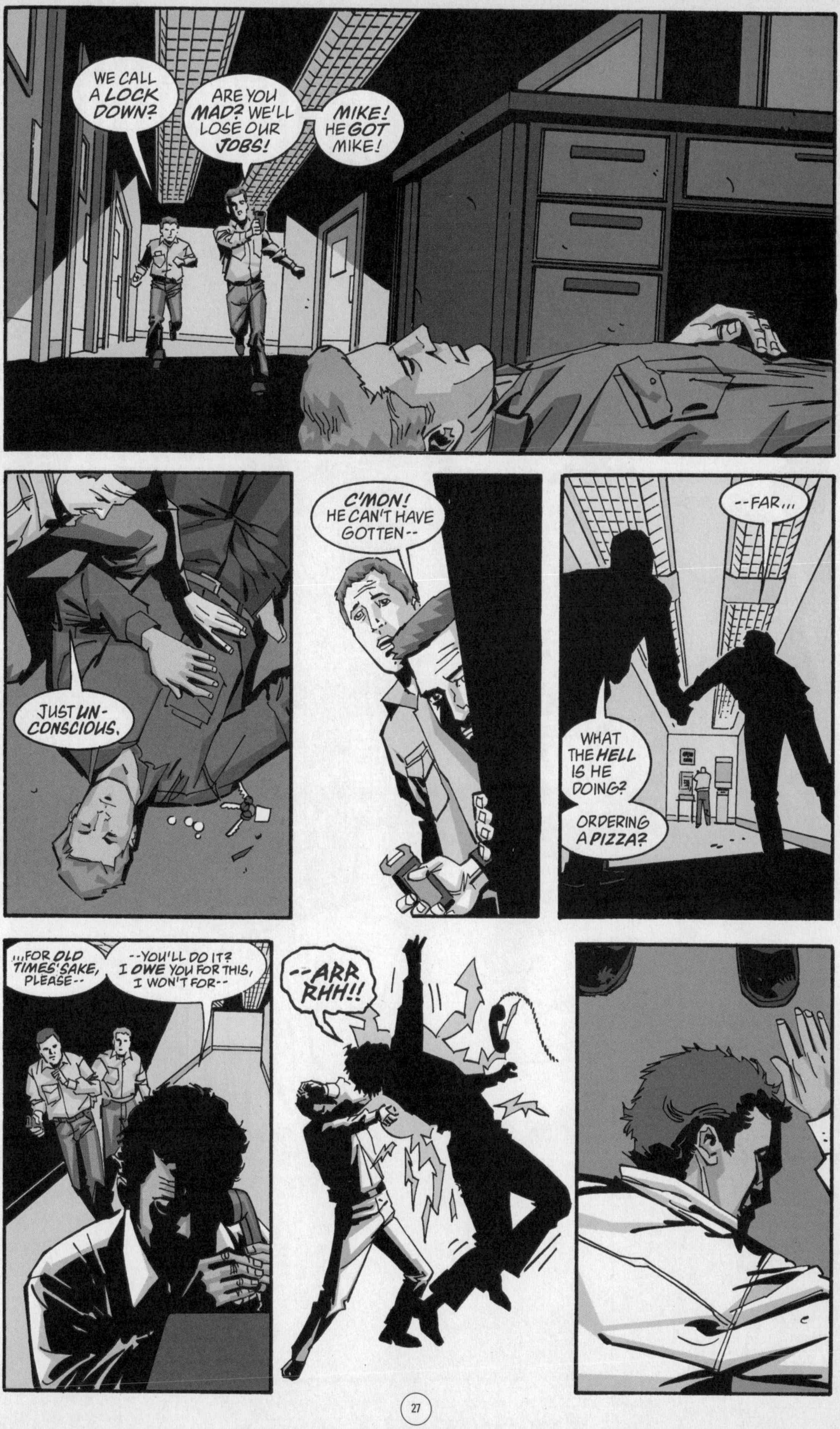

WE CALL A LOCK DOWN?
ARE YOU MAD? WE'LL LOSE OUR JOBS!
MIKE! HE GOT MIKE!
JUST UN-CONSCIOUS.
C'MON! HE CAN'T HAVE GOTTEN--
--FAR...
WHAT THE HELL IS HE DOING?
ORDERING A PIZZA?
...FOR OLD TIMES' SAKE, PLEASE--
--YOU'LL DO IT? I OWE YOU FOR THIS, I WON'T FOR--
--ARR RHH!!

HAPPY BIRTHDAY TWO YOU...

...TRIAL OF REYNALDO MARTINEZ TO BEGIN TODAY.

IN RELATED NEWS, A REPORT BY THE GCPD STATES VIOLENCE AGAINST DEEZEES--

--THOSE GOTHAMITES WHO FLED THE CITY DURING THE NO MAN'S LAND--

--HAS RISEN FOURTEEN PERCENT IN THE LAST MONTH ALONE.

MAYOR DICKERSON, HIMSELF A DEEZEE, SAID A COMMISSION WOULD BE FORMED TO SEEK SOLUTIONS TO THE PROBLEM.

...LOOKS LIKE *SUMMER'S* ARRIVED.

IT'S *TEN* MINUTES BEFORE THE *HOUR* AND YOU'RE LISTENING TO *GPBS,* PUBLIC RADIO FOR GOTHAM CITY...

EVERY DAY YOU DON'T WORK OUT...

...MORNING EDITION IS COMING UP NEXT...

WEATHER *TODAY* WILL BE WARM, IN THE *HIGH EIGHTIES,* WITH A SIXTY PERCENT CHANCE OF *THUNDERSTORMS* THIS *EVENING*...

I *HATE* YOU.

SOMEONE ELSE DOES.

<MORNING, RENEE.>

<MORNING, MR. ESPINOZA.>

LIQUOR

‹....IT'S HER BIRTHDAY TODAY! BE NICE!›

ding ding

‹MORNING!›

‹MORNING.›

‹HAPPY BIRTHDAY!›

‹WHERE'S BENNY?›

‹AT SCHOOL ALREADY. HE SAID TO GIVE YOU LOVE.›

‹UGH, YOU'RE ALL SWEATY!›

‹LOOK AT YOU! TWENTY-EIGHT YEARS OLD! OUR DETECTIVE!›

‹OUR SINGLE DETECTIVE.›

‹HERNANDO!›

‹I ASKED YOU NOT TO--›

‹WHAT? WHAT?›

‹YOU PROMISED!›

‹ALL I'M SAYING IS THAT OUR *DAUGHTER* IS GETTING *OLDER*...›

‹...THAT MAYBE IT'S *TIME* RENEE STARTED THINKING ABOUT A *FAMILY* OF HER *OWN*.›

‹SHE'S ALMOST *THIRTY!*›

‹SHE JUST HASN'T *FOUND* THE RIGHT PERSON...›

DELI

‹...SOMEONE WHO *LOVES* HER!›

‹MAYBE THE *PROBLEM* IS THAT SHE *ISN'T* LOOKING!›

‹HOW IS SHE SUPPOSED TO *MEET A NICE MAN*, LOUISA?›

‹SHE'S A *POLICE*, SHE ONLY MEETS *SCUM* AND *LUNATICS!*›

‹RENEE DOES *IMPORTANT* WORK! SHE'S *GOOD* AT HER *JOB*—›

ding ding

...TELL ME HOW TO RUN MY INVESTIGATION!

INVESTIGATION? DETECTIVE DEL ARRAZIO, YOU WOULDN'T KNOW AN INVESTIGATION IF IT BIT YOU ON YOUR--

THROTTLE DOWN, CRISPUS!

ME? TELL YOUR PARTNER TO STAY OUT OF MY WAY!

TAKES MY SUSPECT INTO THE BOX I'LL TELL HIM WHATEVER...

MORNING, CRISPUS.

HUH?

YEAH, WHATEVER.

WHAT'S THIS?

DETECTIVE SECOND GRADE R. MONTOYA

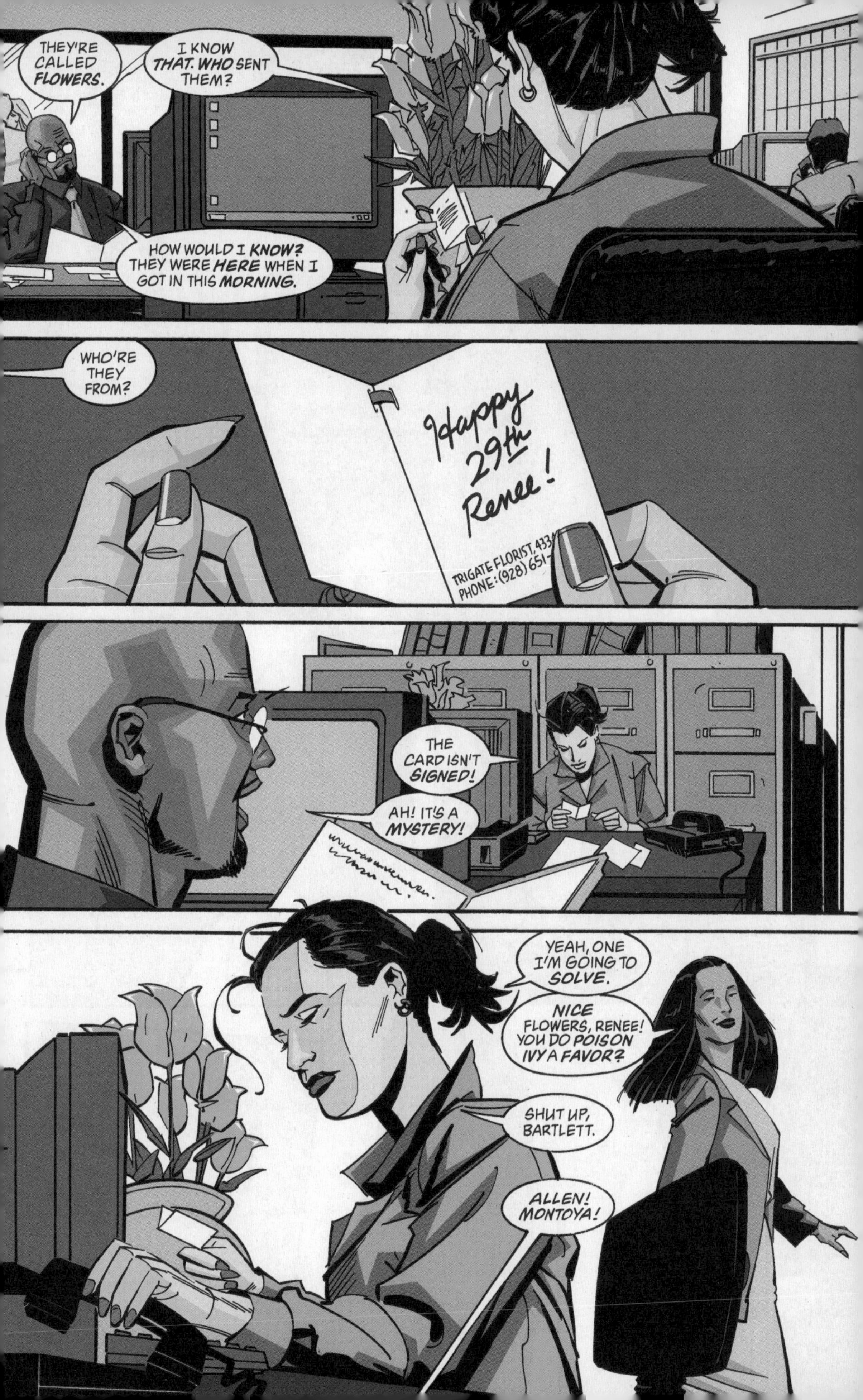
THEY'RE CALLED FLOWERS.
I KNOW THAT. WHO SENT THEM?
HOW WOULD I KNOW? THEY WERE HERE WHEN I GOT IN THIS MORNING.
WHO'RE THEY FROM?
Happy 29th Renee!
TRIGATE FLORIST, 433
PHONE: (928) 651-
THE CARD ISN'T SIGNED!
AH! IT'S A MYSTERY!
YEAH, ONE I'M GOING TO SOLVE.
NICE FLOWERS, RENEE! YOU DO POISON IVY A FAVOR?
SHUT UP, BARTLETT.
ALLEN! MONTOYA!

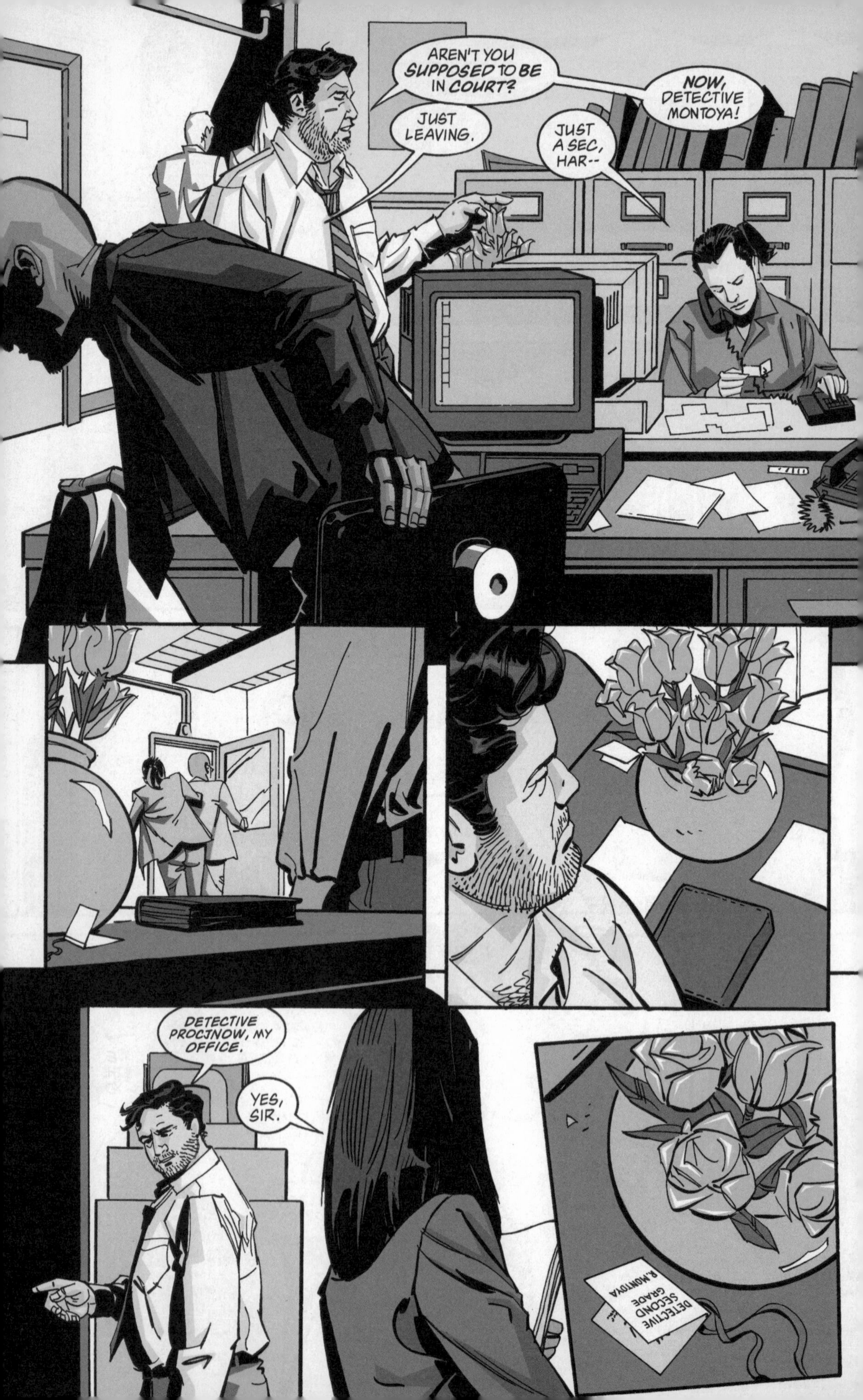
AREN'T YOU SUPPOSED TO BE IN COURT?
NOW, DETECTIVE MONTOYA!
JUST LEAVING.
JUST A SEC, HAR--
DETECTIVE PROCJNOW, MY OFFICE.
YES, SIR.
DETECTIVE SECOND GRADE R. MONTOYA

MARTINEZ COMMITTED **MURDER**, AND THEY WANT HIM TO **WALK**.

IT'S NOT THAT **SIMPLE**, CRISPUS.

...BELIEVE **THEM**?

YOU **WEREN'T** HERE DURING THE **NML**. YOU DON'T KNOW WHAT IT WAS **LIKE**.

IT **IS** THAT SIMPLE, RENEE.

MARTINEZ STABBED BLAKE **FOUR TIMES**. THAT'S MURDER.

BLAKE WAS **FORCIBLY** EVICTING MARTINEZ FROM HIS **HOME**--

BLAKE'S **HOME**! JUST BECAUSE HE WAS **SMART** ENOUGH TO HAVE **LEFT** DOESN'T MEAN HE'D GIVEN **THAT** UP!

WE PAID FOR OUR HOMES!

WHAT DID YOU PAY?

NOT MURDER-- SELF-DEFENSE!

O.G. MUST GO FREE

FREE REYNALDO MARTINE NOW!

WHY'D YOU GET **FLOWERS**?

UH.... TODAY'S MY B1--

DETECTIVE MONTOYA? THEY'VE **CALLED** YOU.

DID THE DEFENDANT TELL YOU *WHY* HE ATTACKED MR. BLAKE?

HE SAID HE *WAS DEFENDING* HIS HOME AND PROPERTY.

THOSE WERE HIS WORDS?

YES, MA'AM.

DOES THE DEFENDANT *OWN* THE PROPERTY IN QUESTION?

NO, THE *DEED* TO THE HOUSE AND THE LOT WERE HELD BY CAMERON BLAKE.

ONE MORE QUESTION, DETECTIVE.

IS THIS THE *KNIFE* YOU TOOK FROM MR. MARTINEZ WHEN YOU ARRESTED HIM?

YES IT IS.

THANK YOU, DETECTIVE MONTOYA.

YOUR WITNESS.

HOW *LONG* HAD MR. MARTINEZ BEEN IN THE HOUSE IN QUESTION?

SINCE THE *START* OF NO MAN'S LAND.

DETECTIVE... ARE YOU--WHAT'S IT CALLED--AN O.G.? AN "ORIGINAL GOTHAMITE"?

I WAS BORN AND RAISED HERE. MY PARENTS CAME FROM THE DOMINICAN REPUBLIC.

I SEE. AND DID YOU REMAIN IN GOTHAM DURING THE NO MAN'S LAND?

OBJECTION!

APPROACH.

GOES TO UNDERSTANDING THE DEFENDANT'S STATE OF MIND, YOUR HONOR. IT'S THE HEART OF THE SELF-DEFENSE PLEA.

THEN PUT THE DEFENDANT ON THE STAND.

I AGREE WITH MS. WILLIS. OBJECTION SUSTAINED.

NO FURTHER QUESTIONS.

YOU MAY STEP DOWN, DETECTIVE.

THE PEOPLE CALL CHARLOTTE BLAKE...

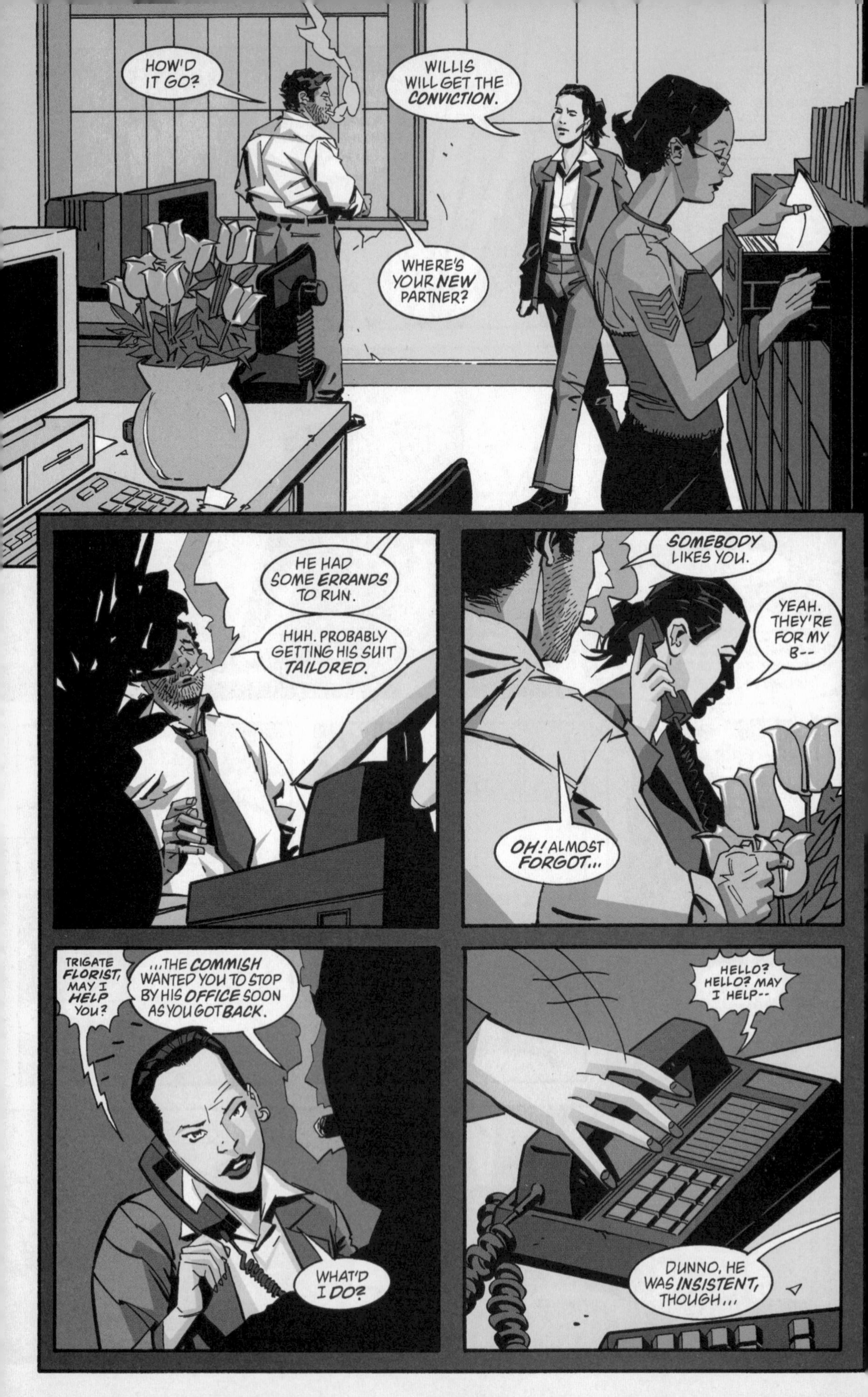
HOW'D IT GO?
WILLIS WILL GET THE CONVICTION.
WHERE'S YOUR NEW PARTNER?
HE HAD SOME ERRANDS TO RUN.
HUH. PROBABLY GETTING HIS SUIT TAILORED.
SOMEBODY LIKES YOU.
YEAH. THEY'RE FOR MY B--
OH! ALMOST FORGOT...
TRIGATE FLORIST, MAY I HELP YOU?
...THE COMMISH WANTED YOU TO STOP BY HIS OFFICE SOON AS YOU GOT BACK.
WHAT'D I DO?
HELLO? HELLO? MAY I HELP--
DUNNO, HE WAS INSISTENT, THOUGH...

"...YOU DON'T WANT TO KEEP HIM *WAITING*."

JAMES GORDON
COMMISSIONER OF POLICE

YOU WANTED TO SEE ME, SIR?

WHAT KEPT YOU?

I HAD TO *TESTIFY*--

NEVER MIND.

HERE.

HAPPY BIRTHDAY, RENEE.

THANKS...

...THANK YOU, SIR...

RENEE? WHAT'S WRONG?

I'M ...I'M NOT HAVING A VERY GOOD BIRTHDAY, SIR.

YOU WANT TO *TELL* ME ABOUT IT?

IT'S NOT *ANY ONE THING* IN PARTICULAR...

I MEAN, MY *FATHER* WANTS TO KNOW WHY I'M NOT *MARRIED* WITH *KIDS* YET...

...MY *NEW PARTNER* IS AN *ARROGANT* PAIN IN *MY BUTT*...

...AND I JUST HELPED THE *D.A.* PUT A *MAN* IN *PRISON* WHO MAYBE *DOESN'T* DESERVE IT...

...BUT *YOU*... YOU *REMEMBERED* MY *BIRTHDAY.*

YOU'RE TOO *YOUNG* TO FEEL *OLD* AND *LONELY*, RENEE.

I KNOW. BUT I DO.

YOU WANT MY *ADVICE*? TAKE THE *REST* OF THE DAY *OFF...*

"...DO SOMETHING FOR *YOURSELF*."

THE CARD WASN'T *SIGNED*.

WENT OUT *THIS* MORNING?

...ABOUT A *BOUQUET* OF *TULIPS*...

FLORIST

YES.

NORMALLY I'D SAY *ANONYMOUS* FLOWERS ARE *SUPPOSED* TO BE A *MYSTERY*...

...BUT YOU BEING A *DETECTIVE*, I GUESS THAT MEANS YOU'RE ALLOWED TO *SOLVE* IT.

Flowers

I *APPRECIATE* IT, SIR.

OH! HEH, HEH... *SONOFAGUN*...

...HE'S SENDING *YOU* FLOWERS, I'D SAY YOU'VE GOT YOUR-SELF *QUITE* A *CATCH*.

...VERY BUSY RIGHT NOW.

FINE.

MA'AM! YOU CAN'T JUST BARGE--

WAYNE ENTERPRISE

--IN THERE!

WAYNE!

FIONA, CAN YOU GET SOMEONE FROM MAINTENANCE? IT'S TOO DARK IN HERE.

UHM... YEAH?

WHY'D YOU SEND ME FLOWERS?

UM...BECAUSE YOU'RE A HOTTIE?

YOU DON'T KNOW ME!

I'M NOT SURE HOW THAT'S RELEVANT.

WHAT'S THE MATTER? YOU DON'T LIKE THEM?

NO, I LIKE THEM FINE!

BUT I DON'T BELIEVE YOU WANT TO DATE A COP INSTEAD OF THAT PARADE OF STARLETS YOU'VE GOT LINED UP.

YOU WOUND ME, DETECTIVE MONTOYA.

WAS IT DENT? DID HE PUT YOU UP TO THIS?

WHAT IF IT WAS?

TULIPS. OF COURSE IT WAS DENT.

YOU DIDN'T ANSWER MY QUESTION.

43

YOU *DIDN'T* ANSWER *MINE!*

YES.

HARVEY *KNEW* TODAY WAS *YOUR* BIRTHDAY, DETECTIVE.

HE CALLED, ASKED THAT I SEND YOU THE FLOWERS. HE ASKED FOR *OLD TIMES'* SAKE.

WE WERE *FRIENDS,* ONCE.

THANKS FOR YOUR TIME, MR. WAYNE.

SORRY FOR THE *INTERRUPTION.*

NO TROUBLE.

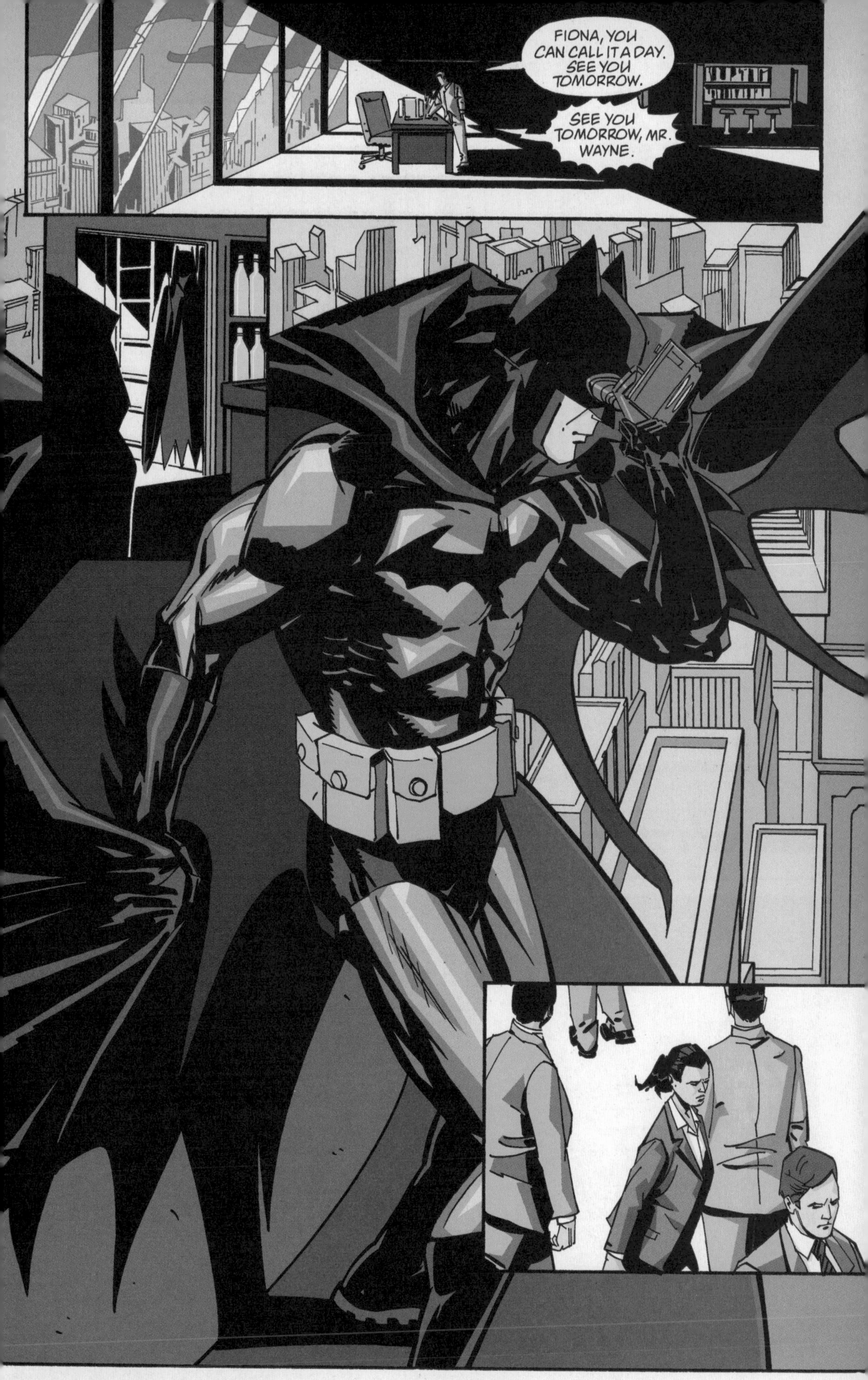
FIONA, YOU CAN CALL IT A DAY. SEE YOU TOMORROW.
SEE YOU TOMORROW, MR. WAYNE.

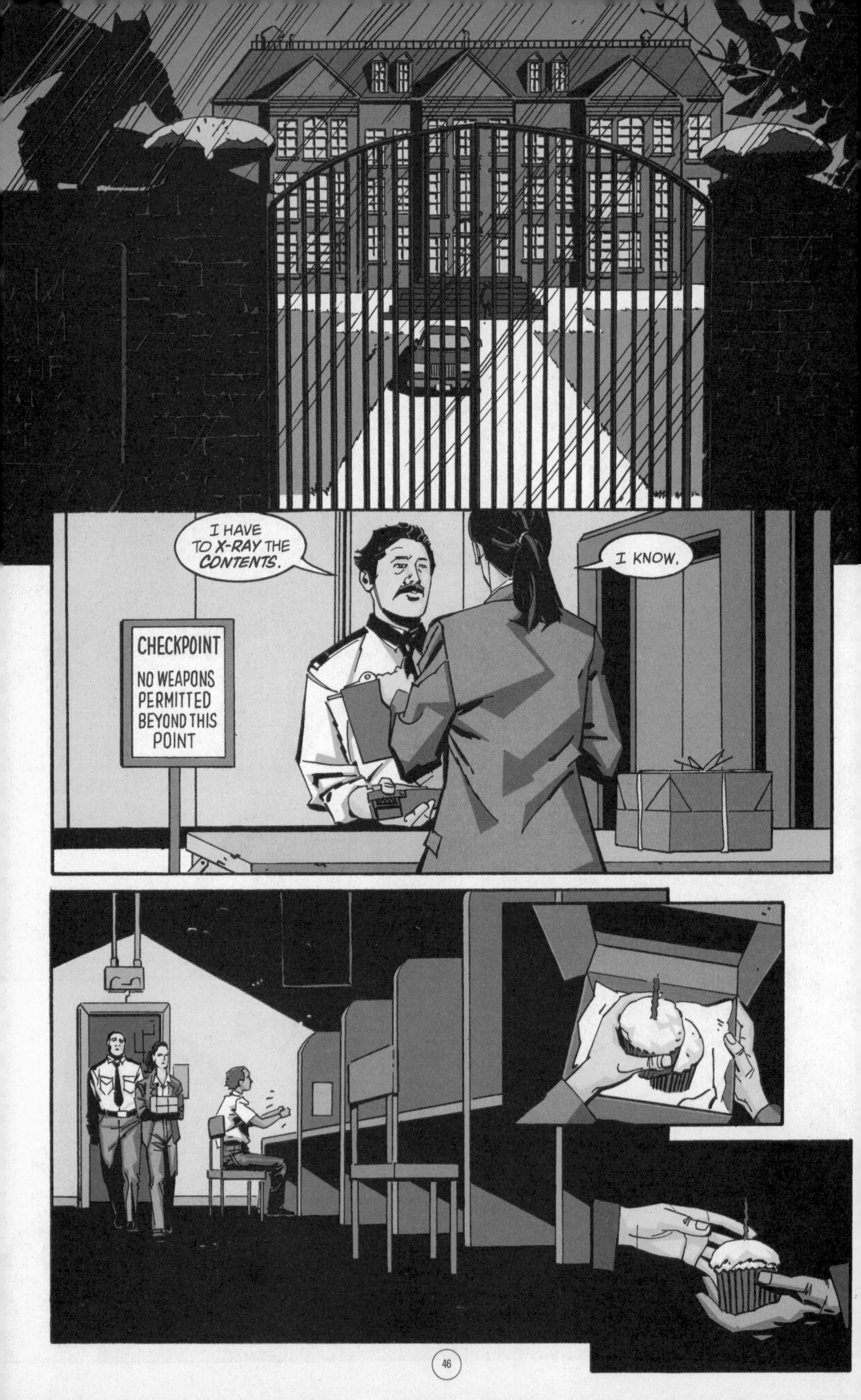
I HAVE TO X-RAY THE CONTENTS.
I KNOW.
CHECKPOINT
NO WEAPONS PERMITTED BEYOND THIS POINT

HAPPY BIRTHDAY, RENEE.

THANKS FOR THE FLOWERS.

WHAT HAPPENED TO YOU?

GOT A *BEATING* FOR USING THE *PHONE* WITHOUT *PERMISSION.* IT'S NOTHING.

THANKS FOR COMING TO SEE ME.

WELL, YOU *DID* SEND ME FLOWERS...

You gave him peace. Thank you for that. Happy Birthday.

YOU'RE WELCOME.

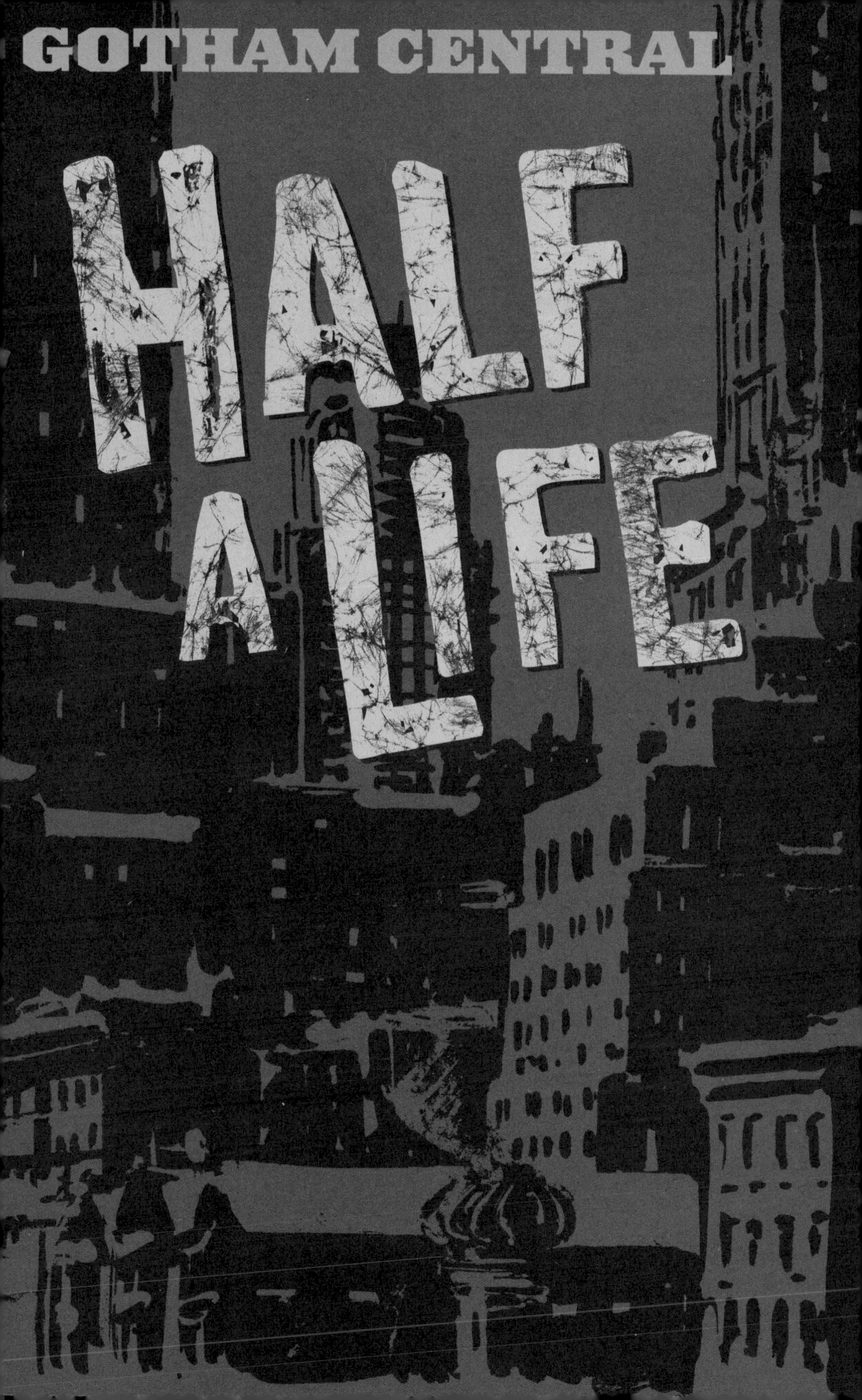
GOTHAM CENTRAL
HALF A LIFE

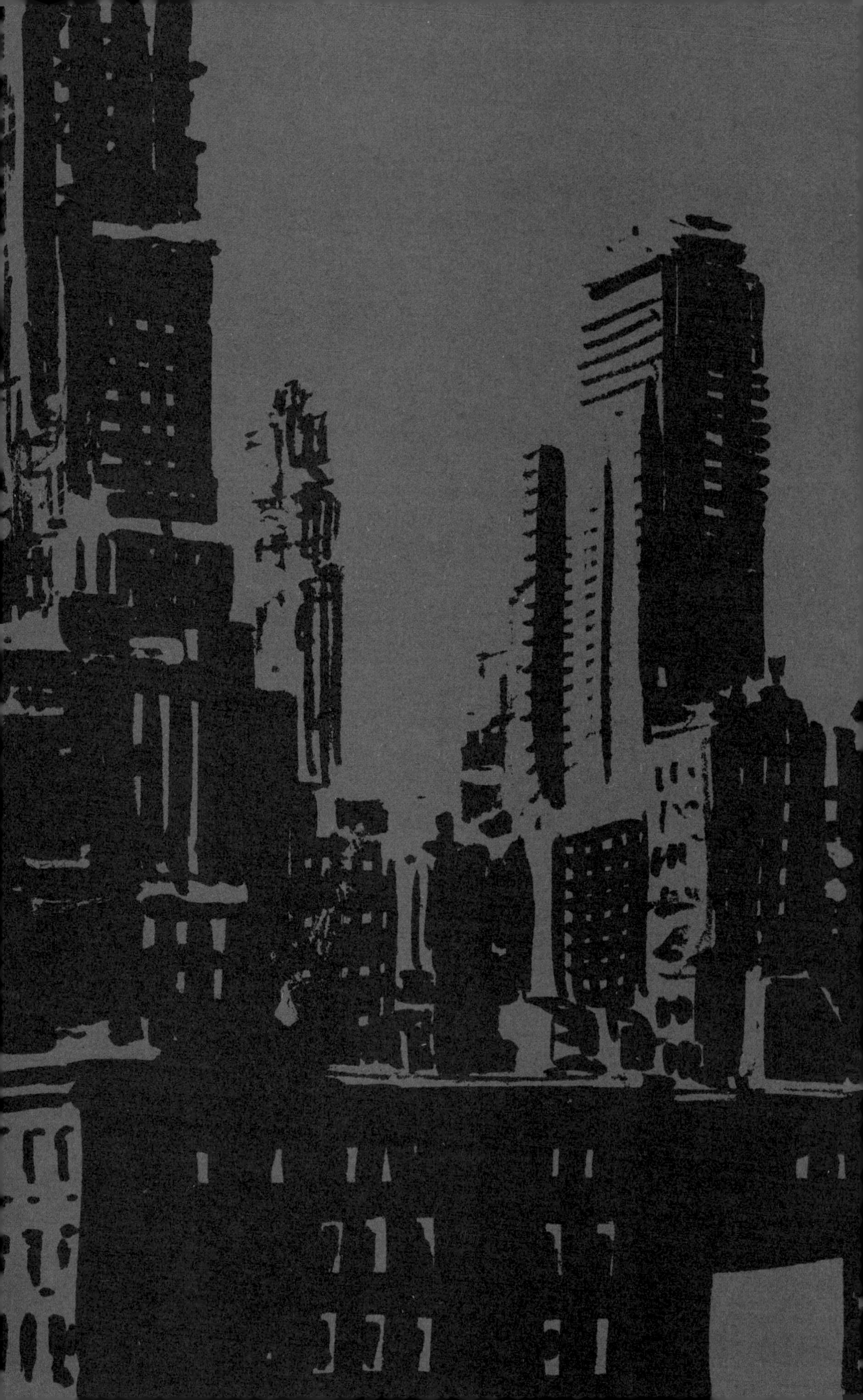

YEAH, *THAT'S* IT...

..."THAT'S WHAT WE'RE LOOKING FOR"...

chk-chk chk-chk c

<MORNING, RENEE!>

<MORNING, MISTER HERRERA.>

<YOU HAVE A GOOD DAY...>

<YOU, TOO, RENEE.>

<HEEL, LEO!>

RENEE MONTOYA?

WHO'S ASKING?

DETECTIVE SECOND GRADE RENEE MONTOYA?

YES, NOW WHO'S ASKING?

RENEE MONTOYA...

...YOU HAVE BEEN SERVED.

HAVE A NICE DAY.

half a life
Part One

...DOWN TO THE OTHER END OF THE ALLEY.

YOU'RE KIDDING.

HAND TO GOD. HE JUST *HOOFS* IT. PURE FLASH ACTION, HE'S DOING THE FASTEST-MAN-ALIVE IMPRESSION.

HEADS FOR THE WALL, HE'S UP AND OVER.

YOU CATCH HIM?

DIDN'T HAVE TO.

HE GOT *HIT* BY A *CAR* THE MOMENT HE CAME DOWN.

DIED ON THE WAY TO THE *HOSPITAL*.

INTERESTING WAY TO *CLOSE* A *CASE*.

WHATEVER WORKS.

GOOD MORNING, MY DETECTIVES.

AND TO *YOU*, DETECTIVE DRIVER, WHO IS *NOT* ONE OF *MY* DETECTIVES, BUT BELONGS INSTEAD TO THE LIEUTENANT CALLED PROBSON.

GONNA BE A *BEAUTIFUL* DAY, TODAY.

A BEAUTIFUL DAY.

SOME-BODY HAD A GOOD NIGHT.

TOBY'S UP FROM METROPOLIS FOR THE WEEK.

THAT WOULD *EXPLAIN* IT.

RIGHT. I'M OUTTA HERE...

...MY *SHIFT* ENDED AN *HOUR* AGO. YOU KIDS STAY SAFE.

THANKS.

WHATEVER.

WHAT'S YOUR PROBLEM WITH DRIVER?

HE *ANNOYS* ME.

WE *ALL* ANNOY YOU.

THIS IS *TRUE*.

I GOT SERVED WHILE JOGGING THIS MORNING.

TOLD YOU EXERCISE WAS BAD FOR YOU.

MARTY LIPARI IS SUING ME FOR DAMAGES TO THE TUNE OF TEN MILLION DOLLARS.

THAT LITTLE PUNK WALKED ON THE EASLEY RAPE, NOW HE'S SUING YOU?

HE FORGET THE PART WHERE HE TRIED TO STICK A KNIFE IN YOU--

EXCUSE ME--

--I'M TALKING HERE-- WHEN WE MADE THE ARREST? SOMEBODY NEEDS TO PUT A BULLET IN THAT GUY.

I SAID EXCUSE ME.

GOD, LOWE, NOT AGAIN.

I'M HERE TO TALK TO DETECTIVE ALLEN, NOT YOU, MONTOYA.

WE'VE BEEN WORKING THIS CASE DOWNSTAIRS IN ROBBERY, DETECTIVE, AND IT TURNS OUT--

NO YOU DON'T, LIKE HELL YOU DON'T!

IT'S A BURGLARY--

I *KNOW* WHAT IT *IS!* IT'S SOME *THEFT* THAT YOU CAN'T CLOSE, THAT'S WHAT IT IS!

SOME *JUNK* CASE YOU'VE HAD OPEN FOR SIX MONTHS, AND NOW SUDDENLY THIS INFORMANT'S COME FORWARD! AND HE'S SWEARING UP AND DOWN, "HEY! IT'S *CATWOMAN* DONE THE *CRIME*," RIGHT?

AM I *RIGHT,* OFFICER LOWE?

YOU AND YOUR *BOUGHT-AND-PAID-FOR* BUDDIES DOWN IN ROBBERY CAN'T BE BOTHERED TO DO YOUR JOBS?

NOW YOU'RE TRYING TO STICK ME-- A *TRUE POLICE--* WITH SOME *MADE-UP KITTY-CAT CASE?*

AM I *RIGHT!*

ON THE *NOSE,* JACKASS!

YOU SON OF A--

CRISPUS, *NO!*

C'MON, LET'S SEE WHAT YOU'VE *GOT,* YOU ARROGANT SNOT!

CALM DOWN!

M.C.U. SNOBS, ALL OF YOU. THINKING YOU'RE SO MUCH *MORE* THAN THE *REST* OF THIS DEPARTMENT.

ALL RIGHT, THAT'S ENOUGH.

HIDING UP HERE, *HIDING* BEHIND THE *BAT!*

YOU GUYS MAKE ME *PUKE!*

GET OUT.

CAPTAIN, I--

THIS IS THE *THIRD* DEAD CASE YOU'VE DROPPED ON *MY* DETECTIVES THIS *MONTH,* OFFICER LOWE...

IT'S A A *FREAK,* IT'S A *MAJOR--*

ARE YOU *PRESUMING* TO TELL ME HOW TO RUN MY *UNIT,* OFFICER?

OR IS THERE SOMETHING *ELSE* YOU WANT TO *SAY?*

NO, MA'AM, CAPTAIN.

THEN WHY ARE YOU STILL IN MY SQUAD ROOM?

THERE ARE *CASES* IN *RED*, BOYS AND GIRLS.

THEY WON'T TURN TO *BLACK* WITH YOU ALL STANDING AROUND.

YOU ALL RIGHT, PARTNER?

JUST BACK OFF, RENEE.

I'LL *TAKE* IT, CRIS.

HELL WITH *THAT*. IT'S *MINE*.

I'M GONNA *CLOSE* IT.

JUST FOR THE SATISFACTION OF WIPING THAT *SMIRK* OFF LOWE'S FACE.

"...BUT THAT WAS *MONTHS* AGO!

WHERE DID YOU SAY YOU WERE FROM?

MAJOR CRIMES.

BUT IT'S A *ROBBERY.*

WE'RE INVESTIGATING IT NOW, MISS LAVELLE.

CAN YOU TELL ME WHAT WAS STOLEN?

AGAIN, YOU MEAN? FINE. THERE WERE *ELEVEN* PIECES.

SIX *NIGHT-GOWNS,* ITALIAN SILK...

"...THREE SETS OF IMPORTED GERMAN UNDERGARMENTS, TWO CORSETS WITH BONE STAYS, THOSE WERE FROM ENGLAND...

"...AND A ONE-OF-A-KIND *MERRY WIDOW,* IT WAS HANDMADE.

ABOUT HOW MUCH IS ALL OF THIS *WORTH?*

A LITTLE *OVER* TEN THOUSAND DOLLARS.

FOR UNDER-WEAR?

WHAT DO YOU DO WITH IT? HANG IT ON THE WALL?

NOT UNDERWEAR, DETECTIVE. LINGERIE.

HOW MANY PEOPLE WORK HERE WITH YOU, MISS LAVELLE?

JUST MYSELF AND MY PARTNER, CORY MARRA.

CAN WE TALK TO HER?

SHE'S IN SWITZERLAND RIGHT NOW, ON A BUYING TRIP, BUT IF YOU LIKE I CAN HAVE HER CALL AS SOON AS SHE'S BACK.

IF YOU COULD.

ANYONE ELSE? ANYONE YOU LET GO?

NO, IT'S ALWAYS BEEN JUST THE TWO OF US. CORY'S BROTHER, PAUL HELPED OUT WHEN WE OPENED, BUT THAT'S IT.

PAUL MARRA?

THAT'S RIGHT.

WHEN'D YOU OPEN, MISS LAVELLE?

ABOUT A MONTH BEFORE THE ROBBERY. FOUR, FIVE MONTHS AGO.

ALL RIGHT, THANKS...

...HERE'S MY CARD. IF CORY CAN CALL US WHEN SHE GETS BACK?

I WILL. THANKS FOR YOUR TIME.

NOTHING ON CORY MARRA...

...BUT HER BROTHER PAUL MARRA WAS POPPED DOWN IN TRICORNER LAST YEAR DURING A SWEEP.

PICKED HIM UP TRYING TO SOLICIT A PROSTITUTE.

THANKS, STACY.

NO PROB.

ANYTHING?

PAUL MARRA WAS PICKED UP LAST YEAR TRYING TO GET SOME.

LET'S GO TALK TO HIM.

WE COULD ASK HIM TO COME HERE.

PUT THE FEAR OF GOD IN HIM.

YOU THINK HE'LL VOLUNTEER TO COME ON OVER?

I THINK I CAN PERSUADE HIM.

CAN I HELP YOU?

YES, I THINK, I MEAN, I HOPE SO...

...I'M LOOKING FOR DETECTIVE MONTOYA. NO, WAIT, WHAT I *MEAN* IS THAT DETECTIVE MONTOYA *ASKED* ME TO STOP BY.

Uh-huh.

MY NAME'S PAUL MARRA, SHE *CALLED* ME--

RIGHT, WELL IF YOU'LL--

MISTER MARRA? I'M RENEE MONTOYA...

...THANKS SO *MUCH* FOR COMING DOWN ON SUCH SHORT NOTICE.

THANKS, STACY, I'VE GOT IT.

MISTER MARRA--CAN I CALL YOU PAUL?

Uh, SURE, YOU--

LISTEN, PAUL, WHY DON'T WE TALK IN HERE...

...WHERE WE CAN HAVE SOME PRIVACY.

UM... BUT WHERE ARE YOU GOING?

JUST MAKE YOURSELF *COMFORTABLE*, I'LL BE *RIGHT* WITH YOU.

HE'S A JUNKIE.

OH, YEAH?

PUT MONEY ON IT.

SO MAYBE THAT ARREST FOR SOLICITING...

YEAH. PUSHERS AND HOOKERS DO TEND TO SHARE THE SAME CORNERS.

CAN YOU FINISH HIM OFF? I'VE GOT A DINNER DATE.

WHAT WAS THAT? DID YOU SAY DATE?

WHO'S THE LUCKY GUY?

YOUR DEDUCTION IS FLAWED, DETECTIVE...

...IT'S WITH MY PARENTS.

I WILL HAPPILY BLOW IT OFF IF YOU WANT ME TO STICK AROUND.

Nah. GO AHEAD.

I'LL HAVE THIS GUY WRITING UP HIS CONFESSION IN FIVE MINUTES.

PAUL! NO, DON'T GET UP, MY NAME'S DETECTIVE ALLEN.

RENEE HAD TO RUN DOWN TO THE LAB TO CHECK ON SOME FINGER-PRINTS.

SO, PAUL-- YOU DON'T MIND IF I CALL YOU PAUL, HUH?--SO, PAUL, HOW LONG YOU BEEN A JUNKIE...?

‹REALLY, MOM, I'M FULL. IT WAS DELICIOUS, BUT I'VE HAD ENOUGH.›

‹RENEE! YOU BARELY ATE!›

‹LEAVE HER BE, LOUISA.›

‹SHE'S WATCHING HER WEIGHT, WE SHOULDN'T TEMPT HER.›

‹IS THAT WHAT YOU'RE DOING, RENEE? TRYING TO CATCH SOMEONE'S EYE?›

‹NO, MOM, I'M FULL, THAT'S ALL.›

‹PITY.›

‹HERNANDO, STOP IT.›

‹HE HAS VISIONS OF GRANDCHILDREN DANCING IN HIS HEAD.›

‹AND YOU DON'T?›

‹ISN'T BENNY SEEING SOMEONE?›

‹YOUR BROTHER IS SEEING SEVERAL YOUNG LADIES, FROM WHAT WE UNDERSTAND.›

‹I WANTED HIM TO TALK TO FATHER RAMON, BUT OF COURSE, HE REFUSED.›

‹HE'S A BOY. AND HE'S YOUNG, HE'LL SETTLE DOWN SOON ENOUGH.›

‹BUT YOU, RENEE, YOU'RE NOT GETTING ANY YOUNGER.›

‹YOU'LL BE AN OLD MAID AT THIS RATE...›

HELL WITH IT...

HEY, IT'S ME...

...NO, I KNOW IT'S BEEN A WHILE...

...YEAH WELL NOT THAT GOOD, ACTUALLY...

...I WAS KINDA HOPING I COULD COME OVER...

RENEE.

AHHH!!!

YOU MAKE IT A *HABIT* TO SNEAK UP ON PEOPLE, INSPECTOR ESPERANZA? OR IS THAT JUST *SOMETHING* YOU PICK UP IN INTERNAL AFFAIRS?

YEAH, WE LEARN IT THE FIRST WEEK ON THE *JOB.*

THIS IS MY *PARTNER,* MATT CONWAY.

MAYBE WE CAN TALK INSIDE?

I DON'T HAVE A LOT OF TIME. I'M SUPPOSED TO BE IN AT EIGHT.

WE'LL MAKE IT QUICK.

LONG NIGHT?

LONG ENOUGH.

MIND TELLING US WHERE YOU WERE?

MIND TELLING ME WHY IT MATTERS?

TAKE IT EASY, RENEE...

"...WE'RE ALL FRIENDS."

SURE, YOU I.A.D. GUYS ARE EVERYONE'S PAL.

I'M SURE HARVEY BULLOCK THOUGHT SO--

--THE DAY HE TURNED IN HIS BADGE.

BULLOCK WAS ROTTEN AS THE DAY IS LONG. HE GOT WHAT WAS COMING TO HIM.

WHAT DO YOU WANT?

YOU EVER HEAR OF A PRIVATE EYE NAME OF BRIAN SELKER?

SHOULD I HAVE?

HE WAS HIRED BY MARTY LIPARI TO LOOK INTO YOU.

WE HEAR THAT LIPARI IS *SUING* YOU.

ALSO THAT HE GOT A *WALK* ON THE EASLEY RAPE.

SOME-ONE IN EVIDENCE CONTROL *LOST* THE KNIFE.

MUST HAVE MADE YOU PRETTY ANGRY. FIRST HE TRIES TO *GUT* YOU WHEN YOU BRING HIM *IN*, THEN HE GOES *FREE*.

IT *HAPPENS*.

BUT *STILL*, YOU AND YOUR PARTNER SPEND ALL THIS *TIME* BUILDING A *CASE*, AND THE LITTLE PUKE *WALKS* BECAUSE SOME-ONE DOWNTOWN TOOK A *BRIBE*.

AND *NOW* HE'S GOT A P.I. *POKING* AROUND IN YOUR *BUSINESS*, AND HE'S AFTER *DAMAGES*.

LIKE I *SAID*. IT *HAPPENS*. IT'S *GOTHAM*.

YOU GOING TO TELL ME WHAT THIS IS *ABOUT*, OR DO WE PLAY *TWENTY QUESTIONS*?

SELKER'S *DEAD* AND WE CAN'T FIND *LIPARI*.

AND YOU'RE *HERE* AT SIX IN THE MORNING BECAUSE YOU THINK I *CARE*?

IT'S A *MURDER*, DETECTIVE.

YOU HAD *DAMN* WELL BETTER *CARE*.

SELKER'S BODY WAS DISCOVERED AT HIS OFFICE.

HE HAD A COPY OF HIS CONTRACT WITH LIPARI ON FILE DOCUMENTING THAT HE WAS INVESTIGATING YOU.

...BUT NONE OF THE RESULTS OF THE INVESTIGATION.

WHAT DOES THAT MEAN?

IT MEANS NOTHING WAS THERE, DETECTIVE. NO NOTES, NO REPORTS, NO ITEMIZED BILLS FOR EXPENSES, NADA.

WHICH LEADS US TO CONCLUDE THEY WERE REMOVED.

YOU THINK LIPARI DID IT?

THAT'S WHAT IT LOOKS LIKE.

AND THAT'S WHY WE'RE HERE, RENEE.

IT LOOKS LIKE LIPARI'S GOT A REAL JONES ON FOR YOU, DETECTIVE.

ONE HE MAYBE WANTS TO FEED WITH VIOLENCE.

FOR THE LOVE OF.... ANOTHER WOMAN IN JEOPARDY STORY.

WE'RE JUST SAYING TO BE EXTRA CAREFUL.

NO MORE STAYING OUT ALL NIGHT.

WE FIND OUT ANYTHING MORE WE'LL BE IN TOUCH.

HAVE A GOOD DAY, RENEE.

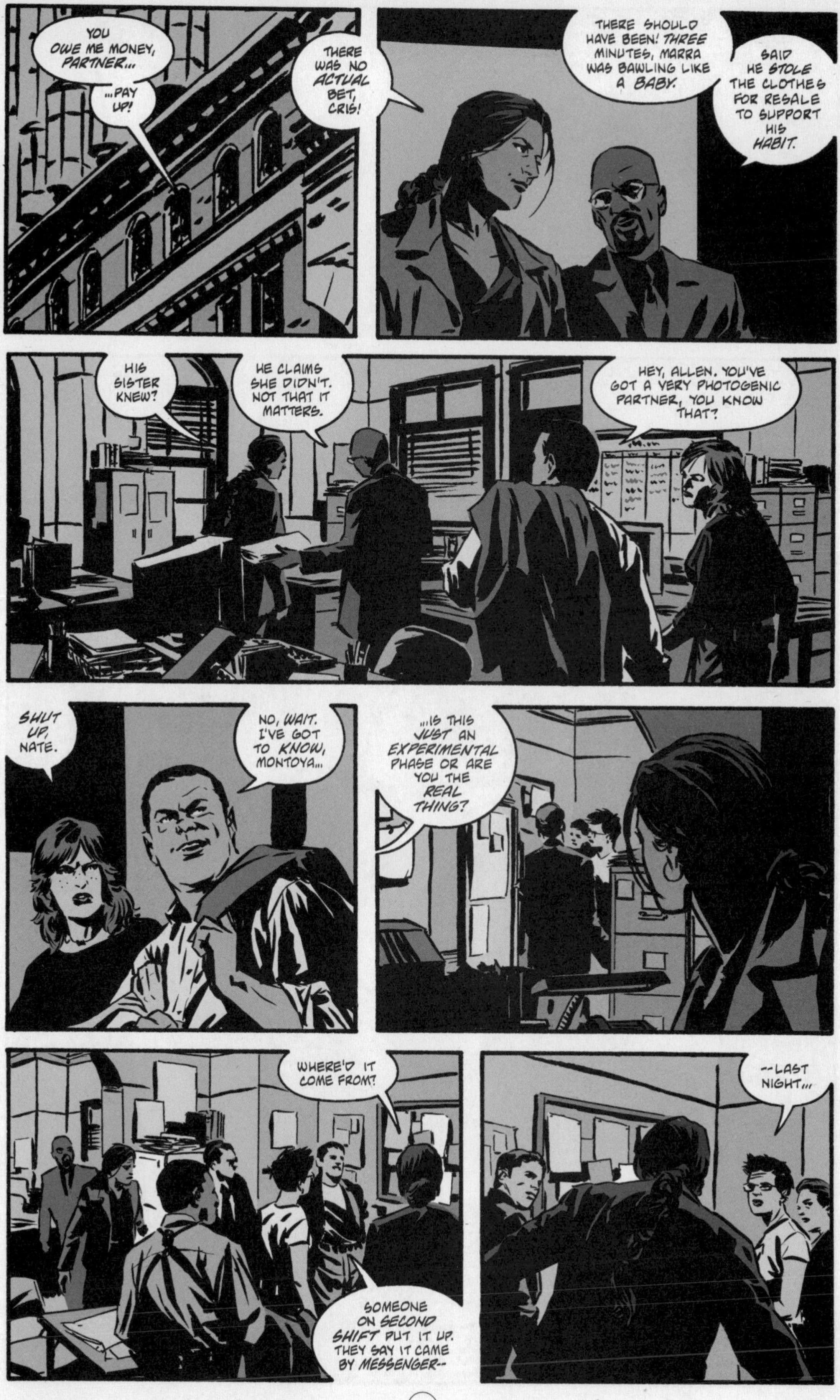
YOU OWE ME MONEY, PARTNER...
...PAY UP!
THERE WAS NO ACTUAL BET, CRIS!
THERE SHOULD HAVE BEEN! THREE MINUTES, MARRA WAS BAWLING LIKE A BABY.
SAID HE STOLE THE CLOTHES FOR RESALE TO SUPPORT HIS HABIT.
HIS SISTER KNEW?
HE CLAIMS SHE DIDN'T. NOT THAT IT MATTERS.
HEY, ALLEN. YOU'VE GOT A VERY PHOTOGENIC PARTNER, YOU KNOW THAT?
SHUT UP, NATE.
NO, WAIT. I'VE GOT TO KNOW, MONTOYA...
...IS THIS JUST AN EXPERIMENTAL PHASE OR ARE YOU THE REAL THING?
WHERE'D IT COME FROM?
SOMEONE ON SECOND SHIFT PUT IT UP. THEY SAY IT CAME BY MESSENGER--
--LAST NIGHT...

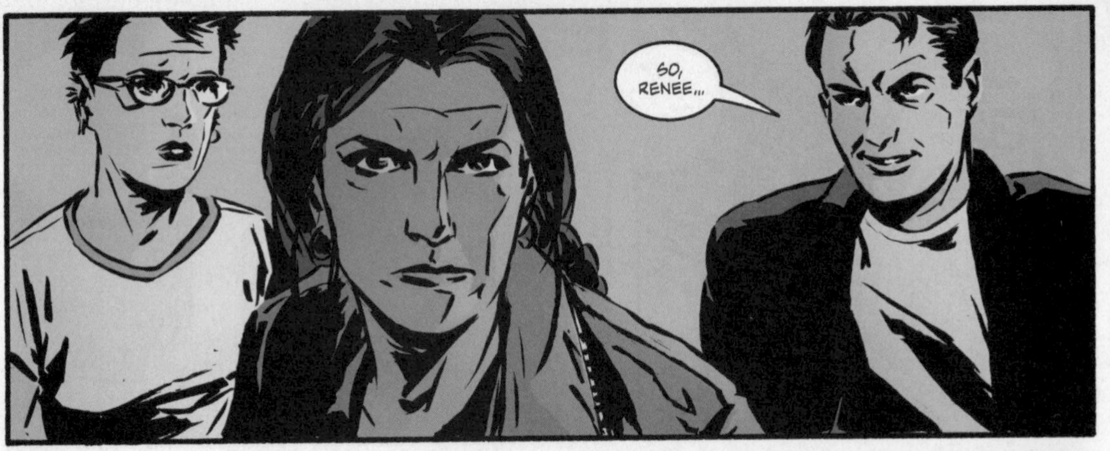
SO, RENEE...

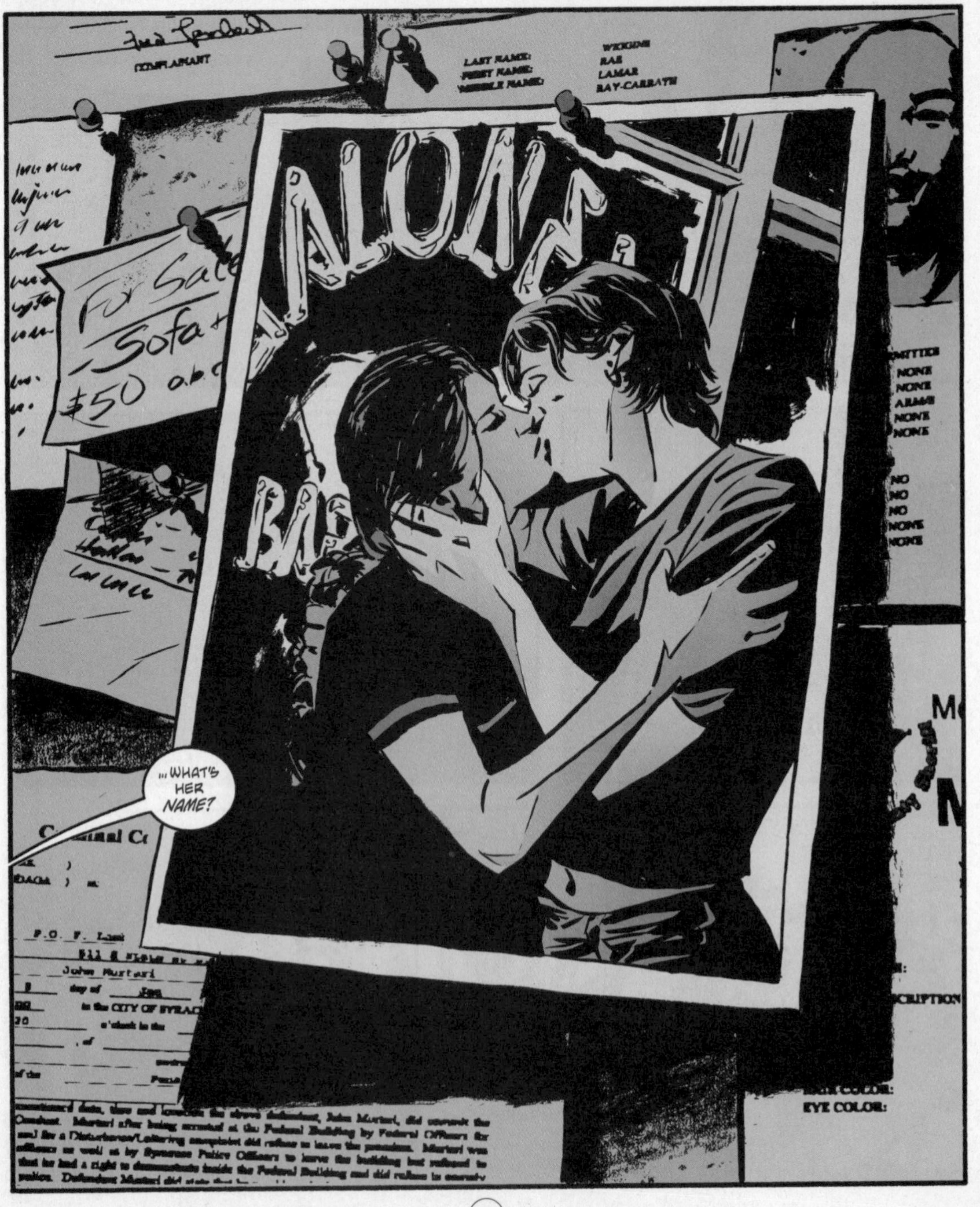
...WHAT'S HER NAME?

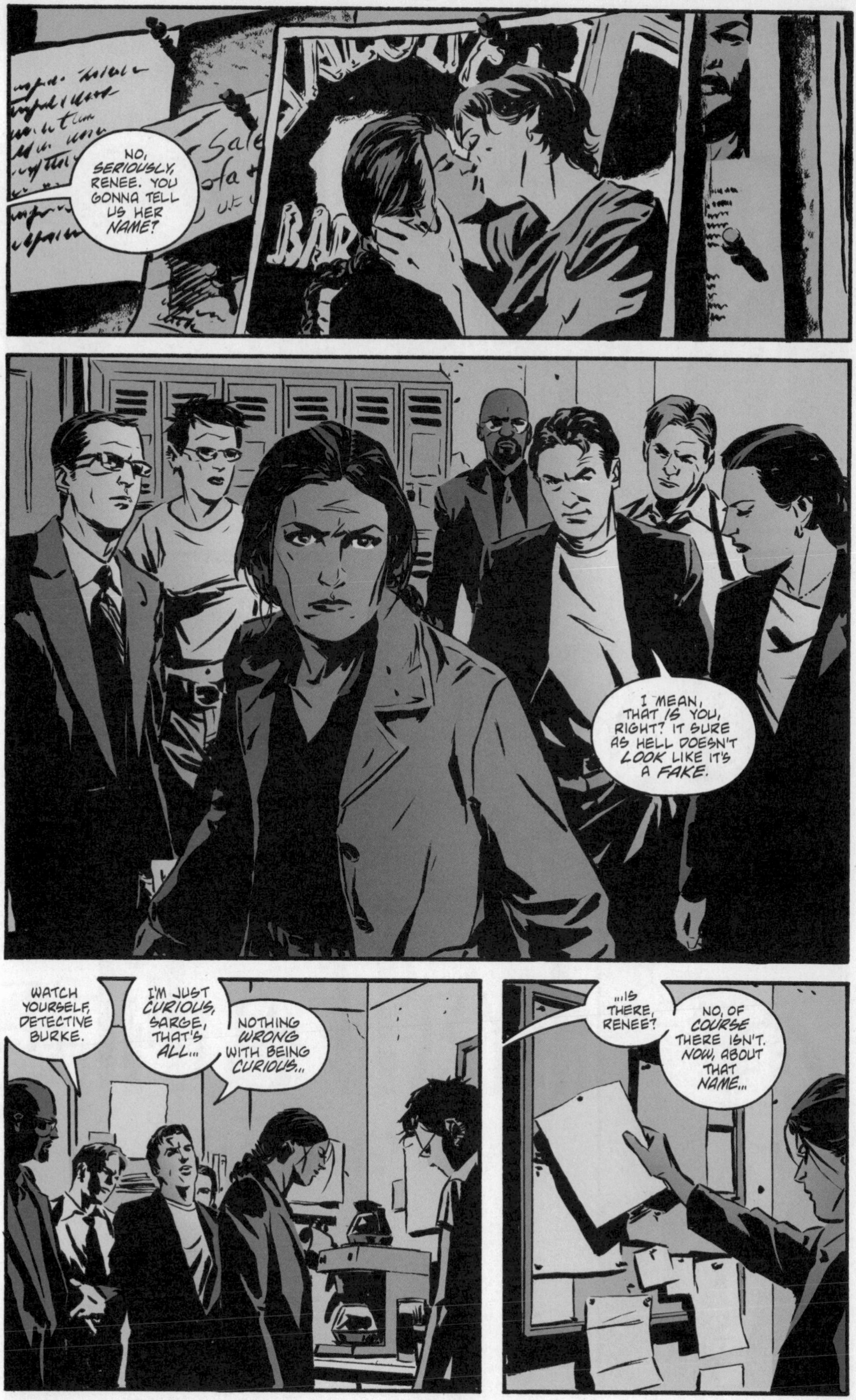
NO, SERIOUSLY, RENEE. YOU GONNA TELL US HER NAME?
I MEAN, THAT IS YOU, RIGHT? IT SURE AS HELL DOESN'T LOOK LIKE IT'S A FAKE.
WATCH YOURSELF, DETECTIVE BURKE.
I'M JUST CURIOUS, SARGE, THAT'S ALL...
NOTHING WRONG WITH BEING CURIOUS...
...IS THERE, RENEE?
NO, OF COURSE THERE ISN'T. NOW, ABOUT THAT NAME...

"... I'M THINKING SOMETHING LIKE MAX OR SAM, ALONG THOSE LINES, OR IS THAT TOO BUTCH?"

TOMMY, PUT A SOCK IN IT.

MAYBE SOMETHING MORE FEMME? OH, I KNOW, I'VE GOT IT--

DARIA.

DARIA.

Huh.

half a life
Part Two

WHAT FILE IS THAT?

CRIS? WHAT *FILE* IS THAT?

LIPARI'S.

THAT'S NOT YOUR THING. HE'S NOT SUING YOU.

YOU'RE MY *PARTNER*.

I'M GOING TO LUNCH.

DETECTIVE MONTOYA.

MY OFFICE, PLEASE.

CLOSE IT.

HAVE A SEAT.

IS THERE A *PROBLEM*?

PLEASE, RENEE, TAKE A SEAT.

I'M SURPRISED IT TOOK YOU *THIS* LONG. IT'S NOT LIKE WE'RE IN THE *ARMY* OR ANYTHING.

WHY DON'T YOU JUST GO AHEAD AND ASK, CAPTAIN?

THAT IS WHAT THIS IS ABOUT, ISN'T IT?

I GOT A CALL FROM AN *ESPERANZA* IN *I.A.D.* THIS MORNING.

YOU KNOW THIS GUY?

HE'S THE ONE WHO NAILED *BULLOCK.*

HE'S STAND-UP, AS FAR AS THAT GOES.

ESPERANZA SAYS HE AND HIS PARTNER TALKED TO YOU THIS MORNING ABOUT THE MURDER OF A *P.I.* NAMED *SELKER.*

THAT'S RIGHT, YEAH. PARTNER'S NAME IS *CONWAY.*

WHY IS *I.A.D.* TALKING TO YOU ABOUT SELKER'S MURDER?

THEY TOLD ME IT LOOKED LIKE MARTY LIPARI HIRED SELKER TO LOOK INTO ME, THAT MAYBE LIPARI KILLED SELKER.

THEY WERE TELLING ME TO BE *CAREFUL,* THAT LIPARI MIGHT COME AFTER *ME.* HE MIGHT BE *VIOLENT.*

LIPARI *RAPES* ELEANOR EASELY, TRIES TO *STAB* ME WHEN CRIS AND I COLLAR HIM, AND *I.A.D. THINKS* HE *MIGHT* BE *VIOLENT.*

I TOLD THEM THANKS FOR THE WARNING.

THAT *WASH* WITH YOU? I.A.D. LOOKING INTO SELKER'S MURDER, THEY COME TO *WARN* YOU ABOUT *LIPARI?*

THAT DOESN'T WASH WITH ME, YOU SEE WHAT I'M SAYING?

YOU THINK I.A.D.'S LOOKING AT ME?

I'D NEVER EVEN *HEARD* OF SELKER UNTIL THIS MORNING.

THAT *PICTURE* ON THE BULLETIN BOARD WAS TAKEN BY *SOMEONE.*

COULD SELKER HAVE SNAPPED IT WHILE HE WAS *FOLLOWING* YOU?

I DON'T HAVE TO ANSWER THAT.

YOU ONLY GET TO DO THIS *ONCE*, DETECTIVE.

TRUST ME, YOU WANT TO GET IT *RIGHT*.

I DON'T THINK I *ASKED* FOR YOUR *ADVICE*, CAPTAIN.

MAYBE YOU WANT TO *RETHINK* THAT.

I'VE BEEN WHERE YOU ARE, RENEE, I'VE BEEN THERE AND IT'S NO FUN, AND IT'S *WORSE* WHEN YOU'RE IN IT *ALONE*.

YOU'VE BEEN WHERE *I* AM? ARE YOU *SURE*?

BECAUSE SOMEHOW I *DON'T* THINK YOU *HAVE*. I JUST HAVE A *HARD* TIME PICTURING THAT.

I HAVE A HARD TIME PICTURING YOU AS A *LATINA*, FOR INSTANCE.

I HAVE A HARD TIME PICTURING YOUR PARENTS AS IMMIGRANTS FROM THE D.R. WHO GO TO MASS *EVERY* SUNDAY.

AND I DON'T REALLY SEE YOU HAVING TO EXPLAIN *EVERY TIME* YOU SEE THEM WHY THEY *DON'T* HAVE *GRAND-CHILDREN* YET.

OR WHY IT IS THAT YOU'RE GOING TO *HELL* WHEN YOU *DIE*.

THIS *ISN'T* METROPOLIS, CAPTAIN, AND *NOT JUST* BECAUSE OUR GUY WORKS AT *NIGHT*. THIS *ISN'T* THE CITY OF TOMORROW, IT'S NOT SAN FRANCISCO, IT'S *NOT* NEW YORK.

IT'S GOTHAM, AND IF YOU WANT TO SEE WHAT THAT MEANS, JUST CHECK OUT YOUR SQUAD ROOM.

SO YOU'LL *FORGIVE* ME IF I ASK YOU TO KEEP YOUR ADVICE TO *YOURSELF*.

YOU THROUGH?

YES.

GOOD. THEN I'LL SAY MY PIECE AND THAT'LL BE IT.

IT'S A ONE-WAY DOOR, DETECTIVE. ONCE THE CLOSET IS OPEN, IT DOESN'T SHUT AGAIN.

WHAT YOU DO NEXT, YOU GET TO LIVE WITH IT FOR THE REST OF YOUR LIFE.

ESPERANZA OR CONWAY TALKS TO YOU AGAIN, I WANT TO KNOW ABOUT IT, AND NOT BECAUSE THEY TOLD ME. IS THAT UNDERSTOOD?

YES, MA'AM.

GOOD. NOW GET BACK TO WORK.

...HEAR THAT SAWYER'S COLLECTING A WHOLE SET OF THEM--

--SPEAK OF THE *DEVIL*, IT'S THE *LATEST* ADDITION.

HOW YOU *DOING*, DETECTIVE MONTOYA? HAVE A GOOD DAY UP IN THE *M.C.U.*?

LOWE.

OH, HEY, I DIDN'T MEAN TO *STOP* YOU OR ANYTHING.

YOU'RE PROBABLY IN A HURRY TO GET HOME TO YOUR LITTLE *LADY* OR WHATEVER YOU CALL HER, HUH?

THE NIGHT TIME IS THE *RIGHT* TIME FOR *LOVE* AND ALL *THAT*, RIGHT?

THAT'S WHAT YOUR *MOTHER* TELLS ME.

DYKE.

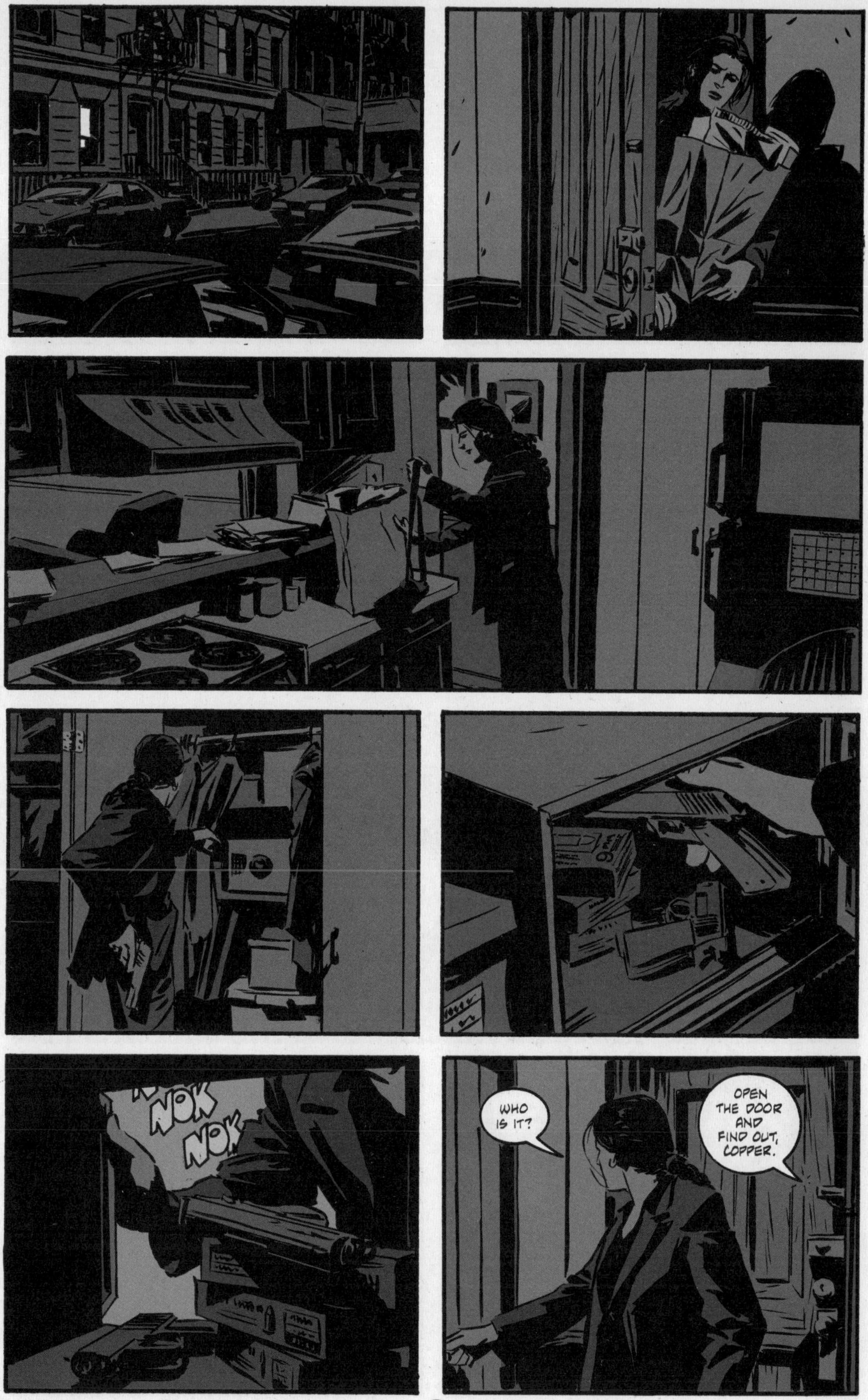
NOK
NOK
WHO IS IT?
OPEN THE DOOR AND FIND OUT, COPPER.

HEY, BIG SISTER.

HEY, LITTLE BROTHER.

THIS *IS* A SURPRISE. COME ON IN.

YOU ALONE?

YEAH. I WAS ABOUT TO MAKE SOME *DINNER* IF YOU WANT TO *JOIN* ME?

AH, NO THANKS. MOM AND POP ALREADY FED ME.

THEY HAD ME FOR DINNER LAST NIGHT.

YOU MEAN THEY HAD YOU *OVER* FOR DINNER LAST NIGHT.

NO, I GOT THE *LECTURES*, TOO.

THEY'RE *PARENTS*. IT'S PART OF THEIR *JOB*.

I ACTUALLY WASN'T SUPPOSED TO SEE THEM UNTIL SUNDAY, BUT MOM CALLED ME AT THE *STATION*, ASKED ME TO COME OVER.

SHE'D GOTTEN *THIS* IN THE MAIL.

SHE WAS PRETTY *WORKED-UP*, YOU CAN GUESS.

DID YOU KNOW ABOUT THIS?

YEAH, I'VE SEEN IT.

SHE'D ALREADY TOLD *POP* WHEN I GOT THERE. HE WAS BOUNCING OFF THE WALLS.

I GOT THEM *CALMED DOWN*...

...TOLD THEM IT WAS A *FAKE*, DONE WITH *COMPUTER*. TOLD THEM THAT IT WAS PROBABLY SOMEONE'S IDEA OF A *JOKE*.

MAYBE SOMEONE YOU *ARRESTED* OR SOMETHING, YOU KNOW, TRYING TO GET *BACK* AT YOU, TRYING TO *EMBARRASS* YOU.

ALL THE *FREAKS* YOU DEAL WITH IN YOUR JOB, IT WASN'T *THAT* HARD TO *CONVINCE* THEM.

ESPECIALLY SINCE THEY DIDN'T WANT TO BELIEVE IT IN THE *FIRST* PLACE.

THAT *HELPED*, YEAH.

I *COVERED* FOR YOU, BUT YOU HAVE TO *TALK* TO THEM. LET THEM KNOW THEY'VE GOT NOTHING TO *WORRY* ABOUT.

SO THEY CAN FEEL *BETTER* ABOUT THEM-SELVES?

YOU WANT TO TELL THEM YOU'RE *GAY*? YOU REMEMBER HOW *FREAKED* I WAS WHEN I FOUND OUT AND YOU WANT TO TELL THEM THEIR DAUGHTER'S A *LESBIAN*?

MOM WAS *CRYING* WHEN SHE CALLED ME, RENEE! WHEN SHE WASN'T ASKING ME WHAT SHE DID *WRONG*, SHE WAS *PRAYING* FOR YOUR SOUL.

POP JUST SAT THERE, HOLDING THAT DAMN *PICTURE*, HIS HAND *SHAKING*!

YOU TELL THEM YOU'RE GAY, ALL IT'LL DO IS *HURT* THEM.

WHY WOULD YOU WANT TO *DO* THAT?

‹MAYBE IT'S NOT ABOUT *THEM*.›

‹AND NOT *EVERYTHING* IS ABOUT *YOU*!›

‹TAKE ANOTHER LOOK AT THAT *PICTURE*, BENNY, *THEN* TELL ME WHO THIS IS *ABOUT*!›

‹YOU MADE YOUR *CHOICE*, RENEE, MADE A *DECISION*, AND IF THAT'S WHAT WORKS FOR *YOU*, GREAT--›

‹--BUT THERE'S NO REASON MOM AND POP HAVE TO *SUFFER* FOR IT!›

‹MAYBE IT *WASN'T* A *CHOICE*, BEN!›

‹MAYBE, JUST *MAYBE*, I NEVER HAD A *SAY* IN THE *MATTER*!›

‹AND *MAYBE* I'M *GLAD*.›

‹MAYBE, BUT *NEITHER* DID *THEY*.›

‹*NONE* OF US *DID*.›

DAMMIT.

DAMMIT TO HELL.

HEY, IT'S ME...

YOU SURE THIS IS *PRIVATE* ENOUGH?

THIS *TABLE* IS ALMOST *WELL-LIT*, RENEE. SOMEONE MIGHT *SEE* US TOGETHER.

THEY MIGHT THINK WE'RE *LOVERS* OR *SOMETHING.*

THAT'S *REALLY* FUNNY, DEE. THAT'S *JUST* WHAT I WAS HOPING I'D GET FROM YOU.

IT'S A *STEP* UP FROM MEETING *BEHIND CLOSED DOORS.*

I SUPPOSE I SHOULDN'T *COMPLAIN.*

I GOT OUTED AT WORK TODAY.

WHAT?

I GOT OUTED--

I HEARD YOU, OUTED HOW?

SEE FOR YOURSELF.

THERE WAS ONE HANGING ON THE BULLETIN BOARD IN THE SQUADROOM THIS MORNING.

THAT COPY WAS SENT TO MY PARENTS.

YOUR PARENTS SAW THIS?

YES. MY LITTLE BROTHER-- WHO INCIDENTALLY HAS KNOWN I'M QUEER SINCE HE WAS FIFTEEN AND AFTER TEN YEARS STILL CAN'T DEAL WITH IT-- COVERED FOR ME.

HE TOLD THEM IT WAS PROBABLY SOMEONE'S IDEA OF A JOKE.

AT LEAST YOU CAN TELL THEM I KNOW HOW TO COOK.

IT'S NOT FUNNY, DEE.

NO. I KNOW IT ISN'T.

YOU GOING TO TELL THEM?

MY PARENTS? LOOKS LIKE IF I DON'T MARTY LIPARI WILL.

MARTY LIPARI'S THE GUY WHO TOOK THE PICTURE?

MARTY LIPARI'S THE GUY WHO *PAID* SOME *P.I.* TO TAKE THE PICTURE.

MARTY LIPARI DOESN'T LIKE ME VERY MUCH.

YOU WANT TO GET OUT OF HERE?

DESPERATELY.

MAY I WALK YOU HOME?

I'D LIKE THAT.

WHAT ARE YOU GOING TO DO?

YOU MEAN ABOUT THE *PHOTO*?

I MEAN ABOUT *ALL* OF IT.

I DON'T KNOW IF IT IS MARTY LIPARI WHO'S *DOING* THIS. AND I GO AFTER HIM, ALL I DO IS GIVE HIM *MORE* AMMUNITION FOR HIS *CIVIL SUIT*.

THAT JUST GETS ME *AND* THE DEPARTMENT IN MORE TROUBLE, AND RIGHT NOW I NEED ALL THE *FRIENDS* IN THE G.C.P.D. I CAN *GET*.

BUT IT'S AN INVASION OF *PRIVACY*. YOU CAN GET HIM FOR SLANDER OR LIBEL, WHICHEVER IT IS.

THE PHOTOS ARE TECHNICALLY *PRINT*, SO IT'D BE LIBEL.

THING IS, I.A.D. WAS WAITING FOR ME THIS MORNING, WHEN I GOT HOME FROM *YOUR* PLACE. THEY TOLD ME THE P.I. --*SELKER*-- HAD BEEN *MURDERED*.

THEY SAID THEY'D COME BY TO *WARN* ME THAT LIPARI MIGHT BE *VIOLENT*.

YOU DON'T SOUND CONVINCED.

I THINK THEY'D SEEN THE *PHOTO* ALREADY, AND THAT THEY WERE CHECKING ME FOR THE *CRIME*, THAT'S WHAT I THINK.

I THINK THEY WERE LOOKING AT ME AS A SUSPECT.

YOU WANT TO COME UP?

I *DO,* BUT I'M NOT GOING TO.

NOT TONIGHT.

I'M AT THE *RESTAURANT* UNTIL TWO, THEN HOME. YOU WANT, I CAN CALL WHEN YOU GET OFF WORK.

I WANT.

GOOD.

I'M DISAPPOINTED--

--I WAS HOPING FOR SOMETHING WITH A LITTLE MORE *HEAT.* A LITTLE MORE WHAT THE BOYS LIKE, YOU KNOW?

THAT WAS *HARDLY* WORTH THE VIDEOTAPE, MONTOYA. YOU WEARING A *CHASTITY* BELT OR WHAT?

I MEAN, IS THAT *ANY* WAY TO SAY *GOODNIGHT* TO YOUR *LOVER?*

NOW *SMILE* FOR THE *CAMERA.*

GET OUT OF HERE, LIPARI.

AW, YOU *REMEMBER* MY NAME.

OF *COURSE,* YOU DAMN WELL *SHOULD,* CONSIDERING WHAT YOU DID TO ME.

DON'T DO ANYTHING *HASTY,* DETECTIVE.

YOU'D HATE FOR ME TO GET ANY *MORE* OF *YOUR* DEVIANT BEHAVIOR ON *FILM...*

...ESPECIALLY WITH YOUR *GIRLFRIEND* WATCHING.

•REC

WOULDN'T WANT HER FINDING OUT *EXACTLY* HOW ROUGH YOU CAN *PLAY,* DO YOU?

MAYBE I SHOULD *TALK* TO HER, HUH? I MIGHT BE ABLE TO *STRAIGHTEN* HER OUT.

AFTER ALL, YOU *KNOW* MY *REPUTATION* WITH THE *LADIES--*

HEY,
SHOULDN'T HAVE
DONE THAT...

rngg

huh

--YOU GO AFTER *HER*, I SWEAR TO GOD YOU WON'T BE ABLE TO *DIE* ENOUGH.

YOU COME AFTER *ME*, THAT'S ONE THING, MARTY--

SWEAR TO GOD.

DON'T *EVER* COME BACK HERE AGAIN!

RENEE!

RENEE, WHAT--

JUST GO BACK INSIDE, DEE.

BUT *WHAT* WAS--

JUST GO BACK INSIDE AND DON'T *WORRY* ABOUT IT, DARIA.

IT'S OKAY...

...HE WON'T BE BOTHERING YOU AGAIN.

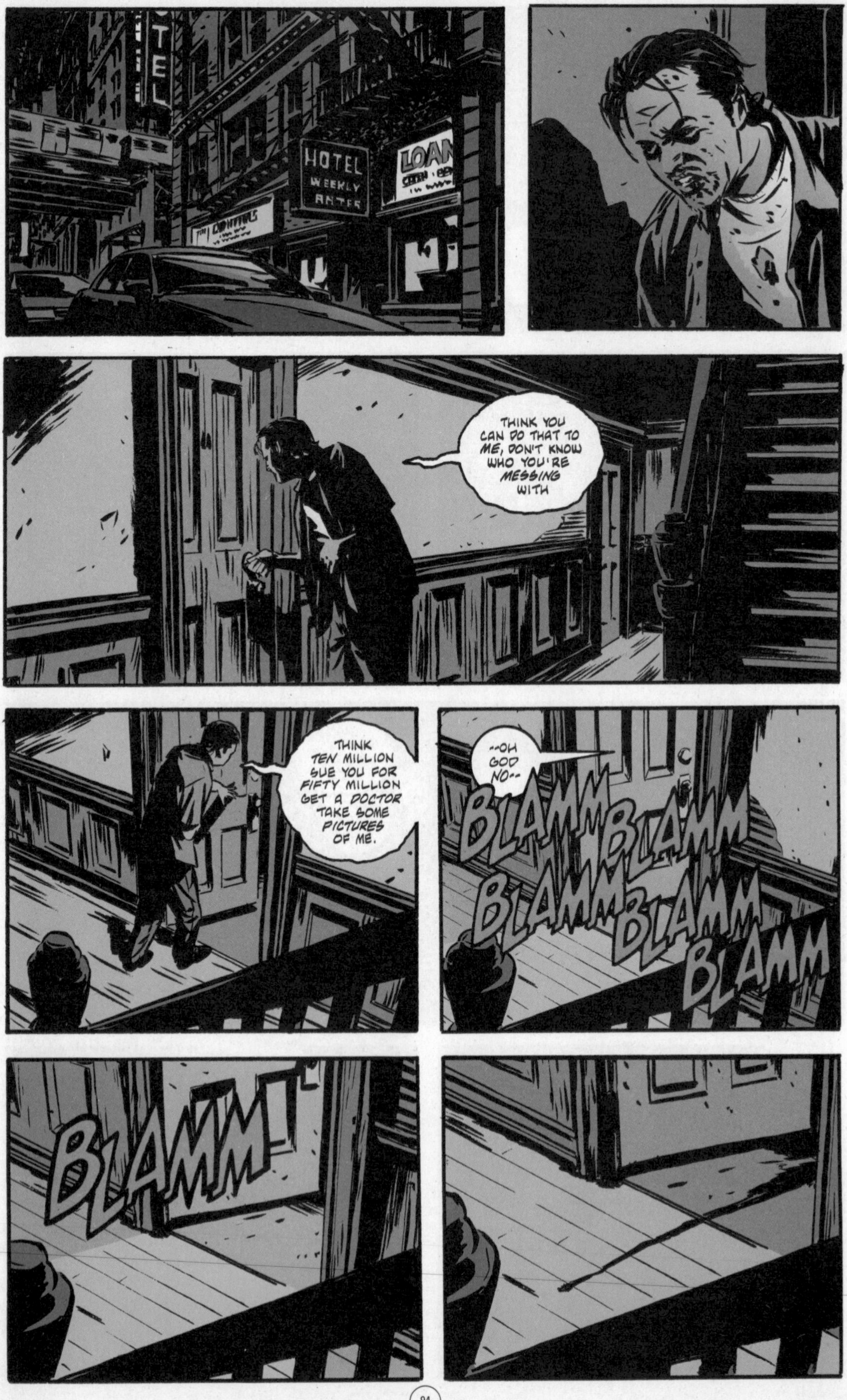
HOTEL
HOTEL WEEKLY
LOAN
THINK YOU CAN DO THAT TO ME, DON'T KNOW WHO YOU'RE MESSING WITH
THINK TEN MILLION SUE YOU FOR FIFTY MILLION GET A DOCTOR TAKE SOME PICTURES OF ME.
--OH GOD NO--
BLAMM BLAMM BLAMM BLAMM BLAMM
BLAMM

WOULD YOU SHUT UP ALREADY, CROWE?

YOU KNOW I'M CORRECT, SARGE.

YOU KNOW I'M CORRECT AND YET YOU WON'T ADMIT IT, AND *THAT'S* WHY YOU WANT ME TO SHUT UP.

I WANT YOU TO *SHUT UP* BECAUSE I DON'T WANT TO LISTEN TO YOU ANYMORE.

M.C.U.

SARGE, *EVASION* IS THE DEFENSE OF A WEAK INTELLECT...

...YOU HAVE TO ADMIT CHANGING THE *COLOR* OF THE CURRENCY WOULD MAKE THE CURRENCY THAT MUCH HARDER TO *FORGE.*

CROWE, THE DEFENSE OF A WEAK INTELLECT WOULD BE ME PUNCHING YOU IN THE *MOUTH.*

BESIDES, YOU'RE NEVER GONNA GET AMERICANS TO USE A *CURRENCY* THAT ISN'T *DOLLAR GREEN.*

JUST WON'T HAPPEN.

WHICH ONE OF YOU CALLED THE M.C.U.?

THAT'D BE *ME,* DETECTIVE HAMMOND.

I'M DAVIES, THE OVEREDUCATED PIPE SMOKER IS CROWE.

HAMMOND. THERE WAS A HAMMOND ON THE DESK AT THE TWO-SIX BACK IN THE DAY.

YEAH, MY *DAD.*

JESUS, I'M OLD.

THIS THE STIFF?

UNLESS THERE'S ANOTHER ONE *HIDING* SOMEPLACE AROUND HERE, YEAH.

WELL TOAST MY NUTS AND CALL ME HAPPY.

THAT MAN LOOKS LIKE MARTY LIPARI, DOWN A COUPLE *PINTS*.

HIS I.D. *AGREES* WITH YOU. THE LIPARI PART, *NOT* THE BIT ABOUT THE PINTS.

HIT WHEN HE ENTERED THE ROOM?

HOW IT LOOKS. THE LIGHTS WERE OFF WHEN THE FIRST *UNIFORM* FOUND HIM, BUT OF COURSE THE *DUMB ASS* SWITCHED THEM ON.

SO HE COULD LOOK FOR CLUES.

HOW VERY CLEVER OF HIM. AT LEAST HE DIDN'T *STEP* IN THE *POWDER*.

TECHS RAN A *POCKET* TEST?

YEAH, IT'S *SMACK*. FIGURE A *KILO* IN THE PACKAGE, ABOUT *HALF* THAT MISSING.

OKAY, GIVE IT TO THE TECHS, MAKE SURE IT MATCHES UP.

NO ARGUMENT THAT IT'S A *HOMICIDE*, DETECTIVE HAMMOND, BUT THAT DOESN'T EARN YOU THE *M.C.U.*

YEAH...

"...SEE, I *THINK* THAT WAS A *MISTAKE*. THIS SHOULD *PROBABLY* GO TO *I.A.D.*

THAT WAS THE *MURDER* WEAPON IN THE BAG?

LAB'LL HAVE TO *RUN* IT.

BUT YOUR *PARTNER*, HE WAS CHECKING THE REG, RIGHT?

YEAH.

SO WHO *OWNS* THE GUN?

HAMMOND, YOU CALLED *US*, REMEMBER?

I CALLED YOU GUYS BECAUSE I'D HEARD THAT *LIPARI* WAS GIVING YOUR *NEWEST DYKE* SOME LEGAL GRIEF.

THOUGHT MAYBE YOU SHOULD KNOW SOMEONE HAD *POPPED* HIM.

DYKE IS A *PEJORATIVE*, DETECTIVE. I'D *REFRAIN* FROM USING IT TO DESCRIBE A FELLOW OFFICER.

THAT *FELLOW* OFFICER IS ALSO THE *REGISTERED OWNER* OF THE *WEAPON* MY PARTNER'S NOW SENDING TO THE *LAB*.

SO I THINK I'M GONNA SHUT UP, NOW, AND LEAVE THE *REST* OF MY FINDINGS FOR *I.A.D.*

THANKS FOR *RESPONDING* TO THE *CALL*.

half a life
Part Three

...LEADING TO CONTINUED TENSIONS IN THE REGION. THE WHITE HOUSE HAS CONFIRMED A SPECIAL ENVOY IS EN ROUTE TO ITARI, BUT DOUBTS FURTHER NEGOTIATIONS WILL ACHIEVE ANY MEANINGFUL GAINS.

LOCAL NEWS IS NEXT.

THIS IS GARY BARTON WITH G.P.B.S., GOOD MORNING, IT'S SEVEN O'CLOCK.

AT A FUND-RAISING DINNER LAST NIGHT, MAYOR DICKERSON ANNOUNCED PLANS TO COMBINE GOTHAM'S FIRE AND EMERGENCY MEDICAL RESPONSE DIVISIONS INTO A SINGLE DEPARTMENT...

...A CHANGE HE CLAIMS WILL BOLSTER EMERGENCY RESPONSE TIMES WHILE ELIMINATING BUREAUCRACY.

PROTESTS CONTINUE TODAY IN CATHEDRAL SQUARE, DEMANDING THE IMMEDIATE RESIGNATION OF CARDINAL WAVERLY AMID GROWING ALLEGATIONS OF SEXUAL MISCONDUCT.

TRAFFIC, AND THERE ARE BACKUPS ON THE VINCENZO AND KANE BRIDGES HEADING IN BOTH DIRECTIONS, LEADING TO DELAYS OF OVER HALF AN HOUR.

GOTHAM POWER AND LIGHT IS CONTINUING REPAIR WORK ON M.L.K. FROM 76th TO 94th STREETS...

THIS HAPPEN TO YOU A LOT? PEOPLE STEALING YOUR BACKUP WEAPON?

IT WAS STOLEN LAST NIGHT, BY THE SAME S.O.B. WHO PLANTED THE SMACK IN MY HOME.

MARTY LIPARI.

LIPARI. YOU'VE BEEN HAVING SOME TROUBLE WITH HIM.

WHAT IS THAT? YOU KNOW WHAT LIPARI'S BEEN DOING, HELL, YOU AND MANNY WARNED ME ABOUT HIM, ABOUT WHAT HE'D HIRED THAT P.I. -- WHAT'S HIS NAME, SELKER? -- TO DO!

BALLISTICS CHECKED?

YEAH, WE RUSHED IT. IT'S HER GUN KILLED LIPARI, CAPTAIN.

PRINTS?

I WISH. IT WAS CLEAN.

SO, YOU DIDN'T ANSWER ME, RENEE...

JUST THE WAY IT'D BE CLEAN IF A COP WAS USING IT AS A DROP GUN.

...WHERE WERE, YOU LAST NIGHT?

HOME. MY BROTHER CAME BY. HE LEFT, I WENT OUT, MET A FRIEND.

OKAY, YOU KNOW HOW THIS PLAYS. LET'S HAVE THE FRIEND'S NAME.

HERNANDEZ, DARIA HERNANDEZ.

SHE'S THE PASTRY CHEF AT XENON.

DON'T EVEN *THINK* ABOUT IT, CRIS.

YOU DON'T KNOW *WHAT* I WAS THINKING, SERGEANT DeI ARRAZIO.

YOU GO IN TO TALK TO HER AND I.A.D. FINDS OUT, YOU'LL BE *EATING* THEIR QUESTIONS FOR A *MONTH*.

THEY THINK SHE'S *WRONG*, THEY'RE SURE AS HELL GONNA LOOK AT HER *PARTNER*.

HOW THE *HELL* DID THIS HAPPEN? LIPARI PHONE IN A *TIP*, SAY RENEE WAS *HOLDING*?

THEY DON'T WANT HER FOR *POSSESSION*, CRIS.

THEY'RE *FITTING* HER FOR *MURDER*.

MARTY LIPARI TOOK THE *EXPRESS* TO HIS *MAKER* SOMETIME DURING THE *WEE* HOURS THIS MORNING.

G.C.P.D. WE'RE LOOKING FOR DARIA HERNANDEZ.

KITCHEN'S THAT WAY.

BUT IF YOU'RE AFTER A *TASTE* OF THE *TIRAMISU*, DON'T *BOTHER*. SHE'LL *CUT* YOUR *HAND* OFF, MAN.

I'LL KEEP IT IN MIND.

SEAN, I NEED THE GANACHE FROM THE WALK-IN.

THE CHOCOLATE?

THE RASPBERRY.

BEGGING YOUR *PARDON*.

MY NAME'S CONWAY, THIS IS INSPECTOR ESPERANZA. WE'RE FROM THE G.C.P.D.

DARIA HERNANDEZ HERE?

THAT'D BE ME. CAN I HELP YOU?

YOU KNOW A DETECTIVE NAMED RENEE MONTOYA?

YES, OF COURSE. WHAT IS THIS ABOUT?

WE WERE WONDERING IF YOU'D COME DOWN TO CENTRAL WITH US, ANSWER A FEW QUESTIONS.

IS RENEE ALL RIGHT? SHE ISN'T *HURT*, IS SHE?

OH MY GOD. *PLEASE* TELL ME SHE'S NOT HURT.

SHE'S *FINE*, MISS HERNANDEZ. WE JUST HAVE A FEW *QUESTIONS* TO ASK YOU.

ALL RIGHT... I THINK THAT'S... JUST GIVE ME A MOMENT.

SEAN? I NEED YOU TO FINISH THIS SHEET, THEN THE MOUSSE.

I SHOULD BE BACK SOON.

YEAH, IT WON'T TAKE *LONG*. WE PROMISE.

106

SORRY ABOUT THE *WAIT.*

THE *POSSESSION* IS *BOGUS,* CONWAY. WHY ARE YOU *STRINGING ME* ALONG LIKE *THIS?*

YOU HAVE MY *APOLOGIES,* YOU KNOW HOW IT IS. A THOUSAND *THINGS* TO TAKE CARE OF BEFORE WE CAN GET TO BUSINESS.

WOULD YOU *STOP* WITH THAT? I *KNOW* THIS GAME, I'VE PLAYED IT A *MILLION* TIMES.

IF YOU'VE GOT *QUESTIONS,* THEN GO AHEAD AND *ASK...*

...*ME...*

WHY IS SHE HERE?

WHO?

DAMMIT!

LEAVE HER ALONE!

YOU'VE GOT A CASE YOU'RE TRYING TO MAKE AGAINST ME, THEN MAKE IT! YOU THINK I'M ROTTEN, PROVE IT!

ALL YOU'RE DOING IS GIVING LIPARI EXACTLY WHAT HE WANTS.

LEAVE HER OUT OF THIS.

LIPARI'S DEAD, RENEE.

KILLED WITH YOUR BACKUP, IN HIS APARTMENT, SOMETIME AROUND ONE THIS MORNING.

LAB JUST CONFIRMED THAT THE HALF KILO FROM YOUR PLACE AND THE HALF KILO WE FOUND IN HIS ARE FROM THE SAME BATCH.

I'LL BE RIGHT BACK.

LIGHT AND SWEET, RIGHT?

YES, THANK YOU.

WHAT IS THIS *ABOUT*, INSPECTOR?

CALL ME MANNY, PLEASE.

YOU WERE WITH RENEE LAST NIGHT?

WHY?

WE'RE TRYING TO *ACCOUNT* FOR HER MOVEMENTS. YOU COULD BE A BIG HELP TO US, YOU JUST TOLD US WHAT YOU KNOW.

IS SHE IN TROUBLE?

YEAH, MISS HERNANDEZ. YOU *COULD* SAY THAT. YOU COULD EVEN SAY SHE'S IN A *LOT OF TROUBLE.*

SO YOU CAN *SEE* WHY WE'RE *HOPING* YOU CAN *HELP* US HERE.

IS IT THAT *MAN*, THE ONE WHO CAME *AFTER* HER? LIPARI? IS THAT HIS NAME?

SHE TOLD YOU ABOUT LIPARI?

TOLD ME, AND THEN THE THING LAST NIGHT.

HE'S... HE'S A VILE MAN.

SOMETHING HAPPENED LAST NIGHT?

SHE WALKED ME HOME. WE MET FOR COFFEE AND RENEE WALKED ME HOME, AND LIPARI WAS OUTSIDE MY APARTMENT.

HE HAD A CAMERA...A VIDEO CAMERA, AND HE... HE MADE SOME THREATS.

HE THREATENED HER?

NOT RENEE. ME. I THINK. I DIDN'T HEAR ALL OF IT. BUT THEY... HE MUST HAVE DONE SOMETHING BECAUSE SHE HIT HIM.

IF YOU DIDN'T HEAR, HOW DO YOU KNOW HE THREATENED YOU?

NO, I HEARD SOME OF IT. I MEAN, THERE WAS SHOUTING. RENEE WAS SHOUTING AT HIM.

TELLING HIM TO STAY FROM ME OR SHE'D...

...OH MY GOD...

...HE'S DEAD, ISN'T HE?

STAY AWAY FROM YOU OR WHAT, MISS HERNANDEZ?

DID DETECTIVE MONTOYA THREATEN HIM?

I DON'T HAVE ANYTHING ELSE TO SAY TO YOU GENTLEMEN.

ALL RIGHT, RENEE...

...LET'S CUT TO THE CHASE.

YEAH. LET'S DO THAT.

MISS HERNANDEZ SAYS THAT LIPARI THREATENED HER LAST NIGHT, IN YOUR PRESENCE. SHE SAYS YOU BEAT LIPARI DOWN.

SHE SAYS YOU THREATENED HIS LIFE.

SO THIS IS WHAT HAPPENED, AND YOU CAN FILL IN THE BITS I GET WRONG, OKAY?

HERE'S LIPARI, HE RAPES ELENOR EASLEY, AND WHEN YOU BRING HIM IN, HE TRIED TO CUT YOU. THEN HE SKATES AT TRIAL.

THAT SUCKS, BUT YOU'RE A GOTHAM COP, YOU KNOW HOW IT WORKS. YOU CAN TAKE IT.

BUT THEN LIPARI DECIDES HE WANTS SOME PAYBACK, SO HE SUES YOU FOR SOME GARBAGE BRUTALITY RAP, AND MAYBE YOU CAN TAKE THAT, TOO.

BUT SOMEWHERE ALONG THE LINE, HE HIRES BRIAN SELKER TO LOOK INTO YOU, TO DIG SOME DIRT.

AND SELKER HITS IT BIG. TURNS OUT YOU HAVE A SECRET, ONE YOU'VE BEEN HIDING FOR YEARS.

TURNS OUT YOU'RE GAY.

AND NOW LIPARI KNOWS THE *NAME* OF THE WOMAN YOU'VE BEEN SEEING, KNOWS *WHERE* SHE LIVES.

HE'S GOT A WHOLE *NEW* AVENUE OF *REVENGE.*

SOMETHING HAPPENS WITH LIPARI AND SELKER, THEY FIGHT. SELKER'S NOT THE *BEST* CITIZEN, IT COULD HAPPEN. LIPARI *KILLS* SELKER.

AND THEN, LAST NIGHT, LIPARI THREATENS DARIA. HE'S A *RAPIST...* AND HE *THREATENS* HER.

AND YOU KIND OF *LOSE* IT, AND WHO COULD *BLAME* YOU, THE DAY YOU HAD? THIS PIECE OF *TRASH* THREATENED MY WIFE, I'D LOSE IT, *TOO.*

YOU GO TO HIS APARTMENT WITH YOUR *BACKUP*-- YOU'VE GOT HIS ADDRESS FROM THE EASLEY CASE-- AND YOU *WAIT* UNTIL HE *WALKS* IN THE *DOOR...*

...AND YOU SHOOT THE BASTARD SIX TIMES IN THE CHEST.

AS FOR THE *SMACK,* YOU WEREN'T *THINKING STRAIGHT,* YOU JUST *GRABBED* IT. MAYBE YOU COULD *PLANT* IT SOMEWHERE LATER, SOMETHING.

THING IS, WE'VE GOT THE *GUN,* AND YOU CAN'T *ALIBI* FOR THE TIME OF THE *MURDER.*

A.D.A. GERMAIN IS IN SAWYER'S OFFICE *NOW.* SHE'S READY TO *CHARGE.*

IT'S TIME TO COME *CLEAN,* RENEE.

YOU TAKE A *TEMPORARY INSANITY* PLEA, THE *JURY'LL* BUY IT. THE *STRAIN* OF THE *JOB,* OF YOUR *DOUBLE LIFE,* THE *THREAT* TO SOMEONE YOU *LOVE...*

"...TELL US WHAT HAPPENED.

I DIDN'T DO IT, MANNY. I SWEAR TO GOD, I DIDN'T DO THIS.

DETECTIVE RENEE MONTOYA, I'M PLACING YOU *UNDER ARREST* FOR THE *MURDER* OF MARTY LIPARI.

STAND UP, PLEASE.

YOU HAVE THE RIGHT TO REMAIN SILENT. YOU HAVE THE RIGHT TO AN ATTORNEY.

I KNOW MY RIGHTS.

I KNOW YOU DO.

IF YOU CANNOT AFFORD AN ATTORNEY, ONE WILL BE PROVIDED FOR YOU...

WHAT ARE YOU DOING?

SHE'S BEING *CHARGED*.

NOW LET GO OF ME, DETECTIVE...

...I'VE GOT TO INFORM YOUR SHIFT COMMANDER THAT SHE'S JUST LOST ONE OF HER BEST COPS.

FIVE MINUTES, DETECTIVE.

YOU SHOULDN'T HAVE *LIED* TO ME, RENEE.

I DIDN'T LIE TO YOU. I DIDN'T *DO* IT.

I'M NOT TALKING ABOUT THAT.

MY LAST PARTNER WAS HARVEY *BULLOCK.*

HOW LONG DID YOU THINK I WOULD HAVE LASTED IF HE'D KNOWN I WAS QUEER?

I'M *NOT* HARVEY BULLOCK.

I KNOW. I SHOULD HAVE TRUSTED YOU.

THAT'S ALL I WANTED TO HEAR.

WHO'S SETTING YOU *UP*, PARTNER?

IT'S *DENT.*

IT'S *TWO-FACE.*

half a life
Part Four

"...DOCKET NUMBER EIGHT-SEVEN-SEVEN-FOUR-FIVE-FOUR-SIX-TWO, THE *PEOPLE* OF GOTHAM VERSUS RENEE MONTOYA..."

"...THE CHARGE IS *MURDER* IN THE *FIRST DEGREE.*

MISTER BARKLEY?

YOUR HONOR, MISS MONTOYA IS A *MEMBER* OF THE G.C.P.D., AND AS SUCH CARRIES THE *TRUST* AND *RESPECT* OF THE COMMUNITY--

SHE'S BEEN IN MY COURT *BEFORE,* DANNY, I *KNOW* WHO SHE IS.

ENTER A *PLEA.*

WHERE'S COTTEN?

MISTER COTTEN IS *NO LONGER* REPRESENTING YOU, DETECTIVE. I AM.

RACHEL GREEN. PLEASED TO MEET YOU.

WAIT A GODDAMN MIN--

SOMEONE *NEEDS* TO ENTER A *PLEA* HERE, MS. *GREEN.*

APOLOGIES, YOUR HONOR. I'VE JUST TAKEN DETECTIVE MONTOYA'S *CASE.*

WONDERFUL FOR *HER,* AND I'M *STILL* WAITING FOR A *PLEA.*

NOT *GUILTY,* YOUR *HONOR.*

SO ENTERED--

YOUR HONOR, I'D LIKE TO TAKE THIS OPPORTUNITY TO REQUEST A *HEARING* ON *BAIL,* AND TO *INFORM* THE DISTRICT ATTORNEY THAT WE'LL BE MOVING TO *DISMISS* THE CHARGES AGAINST MY CLIENT FOR *LACK OF EVIDENCE.*

YOUR HONOR!

WE'VE GOT A *COP* CHARGED WITH *MURDER* HERE, NOT TO MENTION THE *OTHER* CHARGES PENDING FOR POSSESSION WITH *INTENT* AND--

MY CLIENT HAS A HISTORY OF *DISTINGUISHED* SERVICE TO *THIS CITY,* YOUR HONOR, AND THE D.A.'S *INSINUATION* THAT SHE IS A *FLIGHT RISK* IS--

ENOUGH. BAIL *HEARING* WILL BE SET FOR THIS *AFTER-NOON*...

...*NEXT!*

I'LL MEET YOU IN THE HOLDING CELLS. YOU CAN *FIRE* ME THEN, IF YOU WANT TO.

BUT I *DON'T* THINK YOU WANT TO. NOT SINCE BRUCE WAYNE IS *FOOTING* MY *BILL* AND WILLING TO *POST* YOUR *BOND*--

<RENEE! RENEE--›

<--WHAT THE *HELL* IS GOING ON?›

<THIS IS A *MISTAKE,* RENEE! THIS *MUST* BE A *MISTAKE*--›

<THAT *GIRL...*›

<...THAT'S THE *GIRL* FROM THE *PICTURE,* ISN'T IT?›

I'M SO *SORRY,* DEE.

119

NICE JOB, INSPECTOR.

NOT *MY* FAULT SHE *KILLED* LIPARI, DETECTIVE ALLEN.

BEG YOUR PARDON.

SHE *DIDN'T* KILL LIPARI.

SHE'S *CLEAN,* AND YOU'RE BUSTING YOUR *ASS* TRYING TO MAKE HER *DIRTY.*

IF WISHES WERE *DIAMONDS,* ALLEN, YOU'D BE DeBEERS.

YOU'LL *EXCUSE* ME, I'VE GOT TO *MAKE* A CALL.

WAIT. WAIT!

YOU'RE *DARIA?*

YOU WERE IN THE M.C.U.?

I DON'T *HAVE TO* TALK TO YOU. HAVEN'T YOU BASTARDS USED ME *ENOUGH* TO *BURY* HER?

IT'S NOT LIKE THAT DARIA, *I'M* NOT LIKE THAT.

I'M HER PARTNER. MY NAME'S CRISPUS.

DETECTIVE ALLEN, YES... SHE'S TALKED ABOUT YOU.

NICE TO MEET YOU.

NICE TO MEET YOU, TOO.

LET ME *BUY* YOU A CUP OF COFFEE, DARIA...

HOW'D IT GO?

AT THE ARRAIGNMENT.

SHE PLEADED N.G. BRUCE WAYNE'S ATTORNEY, GREEN, SHOWED UP, SAID SHE WAS REPPING RENEE.

SORRY, DID YOU SAY BRUCE WAYNE?

YEAH. DON'T KNOW WHAT HIS INTEREST IS, BUT GREEN'S GOT TO BE A BETTER BET THAN THAT P.B.A. HUMP SHE WAS STUCK WITH.

WHEN'S THE BAIL HEARING?

GREEN'S HOPING FOR LATER TODAY...

...YEAH...

KEEP US INFORMED.

DETECTIVE ALLEN? THE CAPTAIN--

IN A MINUTE.

HEY, YOU!

UH, YEAH?

GET YOUR FEET THE HELL OFF THIS DESK!

SORRY... ...CAPTAIN TOLD ME TO *TAKE A DESK*, AND THIS ONE WAS *FREE*.

IS IT *YOURS*?

IT'S MY *PARTNER'S*.

NOW GET YOUR *CARDBOARD COLLECTIBLES* OFF IT, TOO.

DETECTIVE *ALLEN*...

...THIS IS DETECTIVE MacDONALD, SHE JUST CAME UP FROM MISSING PERSONS.

SHE'S *RIDING* WITH *YOU* FOR THE TIME BEING.

JOSEPHINE MacDONALD, BUT EVERYONE CALLS ME JOSIE.

CAPTAIN, THIS ISN'T *COOL*.

IT ISN'T? YOU NEED A *PARTNER*, MacDONALD NEEDS A *VET*.

WORKS FOR *ME*.

I'M WORKING *SOMETHING* RIGHT NOW, CAPTAIN, I CAN'T BABY-SIT THE *ROOKIE*.

SHE CAN'T BE OLDER THAN TWENTY-*FIVE*.

SHE'S TWENTY-*SIX*, AND I DON'T *CARE* WHAT YOU'RE *WORKING*, CRIS. SHE'S RIDING WITH *YOU*.

I'M *NOT* HERE BY *ACCIDENT,* DETECTIVE ALLEN.

THE COMMISSIONER PICKED *ME* FOR THE M.C.U., SAME WAY EVERYONE ELSE GETS HERE.

AIKINS, *NOT* GORDON.

GORDON DON'T WORK HERE ANY-MORE.

OK, LET'S GET THIS *STRAIGHT* RIGHT AT THE *START,* JOSIE.

YOU'RE *NOT* MY *PARTNER.*

I ALREADY *HAVE* A PARTNER, SHE'S DOWN AT THE CRIMINAL COURTS BUILDING, WAITING TO BE *SHIPPED* BACK TO THE SCHRECK.

MY PARTNER IS A *GOOD* POLICE, AND I'M NOT GOING TO SIT IDLE WHILE SHE'S *FRAMED* FOR CRIMES SHE *DIDN'T* DO.

THEN WHAT ARE *WE* STILL DOING STANDING AROUND HERE?

COME ON, MOVE IT!

TAKE YOUR SEATS AND KEEP YOUR MOUTHS CLOSED!

YOU WANT AN *ESCORT*, SWEET-HEART?

GO ON, TAKE A SEAT!

THAT'S ALL OF THEM?

THAT'S IT, MOVE 'EM OUT!

--THE NAME OF GOD--

--EDDIE? EDDIE! OH, MAN, NO--

...IT'S A **BREAK** IT'S A...

chakchakchakchakchak

AHHH!

hakchakchakchakchakchakchakchakchakchakcha

BOOOOM

chakchakchakchak

CLEAR?

CLEAR.

YOU KEEP YOUR HEADS *DOWN!*

ONE OF YOU *MOVES,* I'M SPRAYING THE *WHOLE DAMN BUS!*

...C'MON, C'MON *WHERE* ARE YOU...

GOOD JOB, CONVICTS...

...NOW, THEN...

...MAKE THE *MOST OF THIS* OPPORTUNITY.

WHERE'S THE *DAMN* CAR?

TRUNK!

ON IT.

"...COUNT SOMETHING LIKE FORTY ROUNDS FIRED.

--MANHUNT GOING FOR THE ESCAPEES--

GET A PICTURE OF THIS, SOMEONE, PLEASE?

--SOMETHING LIKE FIFTEEN OF THEM ON THE LOOSE, AT LEAST...

--CAPTAIN! CAPTAIN! JUST ONE QUESTION--

"THE WEAK SECURITY SURROUNDING THIS TRANSFER...

--DOWN BOTH GUARDS AND THE DRIVER IN COLD BLOOD...

CAPTAIN!

WHAT THE HELL HAPPENED?

IT WAS A COORDINATED BUST OUT, CRIS...

"...THESE GUYS KNEW WHAT THEY WERE DOING.

BOTH OF THE GUARDS SHOT DEAD, THE DRIVER'S IN SURGERY AT SAINT LUKE'S.

WE COUNT FIFTEEN ON THE LOOSE, ANOTHER SIX EITHER IN CUSTODY OR ON THEIR WAY TO THE HOSPITAL OR MORGUE, TAKE YOUR PICK.

IT WAS HER BUS, CRIS.

AND WE CAN'T FIND HER.

WHAT DO YOU MEAN?

WHAT IT *SOUNDS* LIKE. MONTOYA'S *UNACCOUNTED* FOR.

NOT AT THE *HOSPITALS.* NOT AT THE *MORGUE.*

WHICH MEANS SHE *HOOFED* IT WHEN SHE GOT THE *CHANCE.*

IT *DOESN'T* MEAN THAT, BARTLETT!

TAKE IT *EASY--*

SCREW EASY, VINCENT! YOUR *PARTNER* SHOULD KNOW BETTER THAN TO *CRACK* LIKE *THAT!*

MONTOYA WOULD *NEVER HAVE RUN,* MAN! IT WOULD JUST MAKE THINGS *WORSE* FOR HER!

SHE WAS THE *TARGET!*

YOU'RE SAYING YOUR *PARTNER* WAS INTO SOMEONE WITH THIS MUCH *MUSCLE,* SOMEONE WHO WOULD PUT *THIS* TOGETHER TO *SPRING* HER?

WHAT ARE YOU NOT *TELLING* ME?

FORGET IT.

WHAT, YOU GOT A LETTER YOU NEED TO MAIL OR SOMETHING?

NO, IT LOOKS LIKE SOMETHING SCRAPED UP AGAINST THE BOX, THAT'S ALL.

MAYBE THE GETAWAY CAR?

YEAH, OR, MAYBE SOMEONE ELSE'S CAR AND IT HAPPENED LAST EASTER.

YOU SAW THIS FROM WAY OVER THERE?

HEY, MAN, PERFECT VISION, WHAT CAN I SAY.

SARGE! NEED A TECH AND A PHOTOGRAPHER OVER HERE! MacKENZIE FOUND SOMETHING!

MacDONALD.

COME HERE.

HEY, LET GO.

COME.

HERE.

C'MON, I JUST WANTED YOU TO GET MY *NAME* RIGHT.

SHUT UP, ROOKIE!

TWO-FACE DID THIS.

WHAT THE *HELL* ARE YOU TALKING ABOUT?

I'M SAYING *TWO-FACE* PUT THIS TOGETHER BUT I DON'T THINK HE DID IT *HIMSELF.*

PUT TOGETHER A *CREW* FOR IT, MOST LIKELY, GAVE THEM THE *PLAN,* BUT HE DIDN'T *TOUCH* IT HIMSELF.

ARE YOU JUST *MAKING* THIS UP, HAZING THE NEWBIE?

THERE'S BEEN *NO* MENTION, NO *SIGN* THAT TWO-FACE HAD *ANYTHING* TO DO--

YOU GONNA *ARGUE* WITH ME, OR YOU GONNA *BELIEVE* ME?

DON'T *ASK* ME HOW I *KNOW,* I JUST *KNOW,* OKAY, MACDONALD?

THIS WAS TWO-FACE AND ALL THE *ESCAPEES,* EVERYTHING ELSE, THAT'S JUST *SMOKE.*

HE DID THIS TO GRAB MONTOYA.

WHY?

HELL IF I KNOW.

BUT WE'VE *GOT* TO FIND HIM, AND WE'VE GOT TO DO IT *FAST.*

OKAY, I'M *NEW.* I'M THE FIRST TO *ADMIT* THAT.

BUT *WHY* IN THE WORLD WON'T YOU GO TO THE CAPTAIN WITH THIS?

I MEAN, IF MONTOYA ISN'T MAKING THIS *UP*--

SHE *ISN'T.*

--THEN WE'RE TALKING ABOUT ONE OF THE *ORIGINAL* GANGSTERS.

...WE'RE TALKING ABOUT A *PSYCHO* WHO REGULARLY GIVES THE BATMAN *MIGRAINES*

SEEMS TO ME YOU'D WANT ALL THE HELP YOU CAN *GET!*

UNLESS YOU'RE AFTER *SOMETHING ELSE.*

WHAT?

YOU *HONESTLY* THINK I'M *GLORY-RIDING?* TWO-FACE GIVES ME *NIGHTMARES,* LITTLE ROOKIE.

IF I HAD ONE SHRED OF *PROOF* TO BACK MY PARTNER UP, I'D BE IN SAWYER'S OFFICE RIGHT *NOW,* SCREAMING FOR THEM TO TURN ON THE *DAMN* SIGNAL, I DON'T *CARE* IF IT'S DAYTIME.

BUT ALL I'VE GOT IS *HER WORD*, AND JUST BECAUSE IT'S *MORE* THAN GOOD ENOUGH FOR ME--

--HEY, YOU *LISTENING* TO ME, ROOKIE?

HEY, MacKENZIE!

MacDONALD.

SO YOU *DO* HEAR ME. YOU *LOSE* SOMETHING?

I... ...I THOUGHT I *SAW* SOMETHING...

THERE YOU *ARE*, YOU LITTLE SON OF A--

WHAT'D YOU *FIND*?

IT GOT *SCRAPED*. WHEN IT *NICKED* THE *MAILBOX*.

GOT SCRAPED WHEN SOME HOTSHOT FROM VICE TOOK A CORNER TOO FAST--

NO. LOOK--

--IT'S FROM THE MAILBOX.

SON OF A BITCH.

STAY WITH THE CAR ROOKIE, DON'T LET ANYONE TOUCH IT!

WHERE ARE YOU GOING?

TO GET SAWYER AND SOME TECHS...

...AND TO FIND OUT THE NAME OF THE LAST DETECTIVE TO USE THAT CAR...

IF HE'S *WITH* HIM DON'T *HESITATE.*

NO WORRIES. DEALT WITH HIM *BEFORE.*

YOU'LL HAVE TO TELL ME ABOUT IT SOMETIME.

WE READY?

Q.R.T. SAYS GO.

ding-dong

WHAT--

NOT A WORD OUT OF YOU.

CLEAR!

CLEAR!

CLEAR!

THEY'RE NOT HERE.

NOBODY'S HERE.

WE FOUND THE CAR, INSPECTOR, THE CAR YOU USED TODAY. THAT WAS SLOPPY, THAT WAS STUPID, USING A DEPARTMENT VEHICLE.

WE FOUND BLOOD IN THE TRUNK, AND IF IT'S MY PARTNER'S, AND SHE DIES, I WILL PERSONALLY ASK TO ADMINISTER THE LETHAL INJECTION MYSELF.

IT'S NOT LIKE THAT, IT'S NOT--

THEN TELL ME WHAT IT IS LIKE! WHERE'S TWO-FACE?

WHERE'S MY PARTNER?

EASY, DETECTIVE!

I HAVE A RIGHT TO REMAIN SILENT.

137

LAW OF *AVERAGES*, KID.

IT'S *ALL* ABOUT THE LAW OF *AVERAGES.*

hnnnn

OH GOD...

...WHAT HAVE *YOU* DONE?

TAKE IT *EASY*, RENEE.

YOU TOOK A *BAD* BUMP WHEN WE *HIT* THE *BUS.*

YOU'VE BEEN *OUT* FOR NEARLY *TWELVE* HOURS.

IT'S *ALL RIGHT*, THOUGH. I'LL TAKE *CARE* OF YOU...

...SAME WAY I *ALWAYS* HAVE.

I'VE GOT YOU.

HOW'S YOUR HEAD?

WHAT DO YOU THINK, HARVEY? IT HURTS.

I CAN GET YOU SOME ASPIRIN.

YOU CAN LET ME GO.

RENEE, THAT'S WHAT I LOVE ABOUT YOU.

YOU NEVER LOSE YOUR SENSE OF HUMOR.

COME ON.

C'MON, RENEE...

I WON'T BITE...

half a life
Conclusion

...NOT UNLESS YOU WANT ME TO, AT LEAST.

THERE'S *FOOD*, IF YOU'RE *HUNGRY*. YOU HAVEN'T EATEN *ALL DAY*, AT *LEAST*, AND *THAT'S* ASSUMING YOU CHOKED DOWN THAT *SWILL* THEY SERVE AT THE SCHRECK.

MAN. I *HATE* THAT FOOD, AND TRUST ME, I *KNOW* WHAT I'M TALKING ABOUT, I'VE HAD TO *EAT* IT OFTEN ENOUGH.

I HAD SOME *STEAKS* DONE, YOURS IS *RARE*, THE WAY YOU *LIKE* IT--

HARVEY...

...*WHERE* ARE *WE*?

STOP IT!

WH--

I *SAID*--

--*STOP* IT! NO ONE *LOOKS* AT HER *THAT* WAY--

--*YOU* DON'T *LOOK* AT HER THAT WAY I'LL *PAINT* THE WALL WITH YOUR *BRAINS* YOU *DIRTY* LITTLE--

HARVEY!

LEAVE HIM ALONE.

HE WAS LOOKING AT YOU--

I KNOW, IT'S ALL RIGHT.

THERE'S DINNER, STEAKS, LIKE I SAID, WITH NICE BAKED POTATO, CAESAR SALAD, A GOOD MERLOT...

...I EVEN HAD ONE OF THE CREW RUN OVER TO THAT RESTAURANT, XENON, WHERE MISS HERNANDEZ WORKS...

...PICKED UP TWO TIRAMISU FOR DESSERT...

...RENEE?

...IF YOU DON'T LIKE STEAK, I CAN SEND OUT FOR SOMETHING ELSE...

...RENEE? SAY SOMETHING, PLEASE. ANYTHING.

YOU WANT ME TO...ALL RIGHT, HARVEY...

WHY HAVE YOU RUINED MY LIFE?

I DIDN'T.

HE DID.

IT'S HOW THE COIN CAME DOWN. RENEE...

WORTHLESS!

SIX *HOURS* HE SITS THERE AND *NOTHING!*

BLAH BLAH NOT MY FAULT BLAH BLAH MADE ME DO IT...

...BLAH BLAH *THREATENED* MY KID...

YOU'RE TALKING ABOUT *CONWAY?*

HEY, CROWE. TURN ON THE *LIGHT*, WOULD YOU?

YEAH, THAT I.A.D. *RAT BASTARD.*

DIDN'T *KNOW* HE HAD A *KID.*

HE'S *DIVORCED.* WIFE GOT CUSTODY OF THE *KID*--HE'S *EIGHT*--MOVED THEM *BOTH* OUT OF GOTHAM TO SAN FRANCISCO.

SAN FRANCISCO! AND CONWAY'S *TERRIFIED* TWO-FACE IS GONNA *FLY* CROSS-COUNTRY TO MAKE GOOD ON THE *THREAT,* LIKE TWO-FACE *EVER* LEAVES GOTHAM.

WELL...WE *ARE* TALKING ABOUT TWO-FACE.

IF HE WAS *YOUR* KID, WOULD YOU WANT TO TAKE THE *CHANCE?*

OH, *SHUT UP.*

FACT IS, CONWAY DOESN'T HAVE THE *FIRST* IDEA WHERE TWO-FACE IS *HOLDING* RENEE.

THEY WERE IN COMMUNICATION WITH ONE ANOTHER?

YEAH. CONWAY GAVE US THE *NUMBER.*

STOLEN *CELL PHONE?*

OH, *VERY GOOD.* YOU MUST BE A *DETECTIVE.*

HE SAYS THEY HAD ONE *FACE-TO-FACE* MEETING, THOUGH.

THE *PRESIDENTIAL SUITE* AT SOME *HOTEL,* OR SO CONWAY THINKS. HE *CAN'T* BE SURE, OF COURSE, CUZ TWO-FACE'S *GOONS* BLIND-FOLDED HIM DURING TRANSIT...

...SO WE'RE CHECKING THE HOTELS, BUT WE ALL KNOW THAT'S A LONG SHOT.

YOU GOING TO TURN ON THAT *DAMN* LIGHT...

...CROWE?

MACKENZIE!

MacDONALD, AND *STOP* SHOUTING--

GRAB YOUR *COAT,* COME ON!

WHAT? ALL OF A *SUDDEN* YOU *KNOW* WHERE TWO-FACE IS HIDING?

NOT ME...

WOW.

...HIM.

DAMMIT, MOVE, ROOKIE! WE CAN'T LOSE HIM--

I'M COMING.

SUDDEN RUSH, MY DEAR DETECTIVE ALLEN? A LEAD SUDDENLY DROP IN YOUR LAP?

THE BATMAN'S GOT HIS IMPERSONATION OF YOU DOWN COLD, CROWE.

I'M SORRY, WHAT?

HE'S THE LEAD, DAMMIT--

--CAN'T TALK NOW, TELL THE CAPTAIN WE'LL RADIO WHEN WE HAVE SOMETHING--

--AND HAVE THEM MAKE SURE Q.R.T. IS ON STAND-BY!

YOU'RE NOT HUNGRY?

NO.

I DON'T SEEM TO HAVE MUCH OF AN APPETITE.

IF YOU DON'T EAT YOUR DINNER, YOU WON'T GET DESSERT.

YOU HIRED SELKER?

I HAD LIPARI HIRE SELKER. NEEDED TO FIND SOMETHING ON YOU, SOMETHING I COULD USE, FIGURED THERE'D BE AN AFFAIR OR SOMETHING IN YOUR PAST, SOMETHING YOU DIDN'T WANT OUT IN THE OPEN.

MAYBE A KID OR AN ABORTION.

SOMETHING YOU WERE HIDING.

BOY, DID YOU GET LUCKY.

BOY, DID I.

145

I SENT THE *PICTURES*, IF *THAT'S* WHAT YOU'RE ASKING.

HOW *ARE* YOUR *PARENTS*, BY THE WAY? I UNDERSTAND THAT BENNY'S BECOME A *FIREFIGHTER*.

WELL, MY *PARENTS* AREN'T *TOO* HAPPY RIGHT NOW, YOU KNOW.

TURNS OUT THEIR *DAUGHTER'S GAY*. TURNS OUT *THEIR* DAUGHTER'S ACCUSED OF *MURDER*.

THINGS LIKE *THAT.*

I *KNOW.*

THEN *WHY'D* YOU ASK?

TO MAKE SURE *YOU* KNEW IT, TOO.

YOU KILL SELKER?

YEAH. I WANTED LIPARI TO DO *IT*, BUT HE'D HAVE SCREWED IT UP. IT HAD TO BE CLEAN.

AND *LIPARI*? YOU DID LIPARI, *TOO*?

OH, YEAH. *HAD* TO DO *THAT* ONE MYSELF.

HE SET HIMSELF UP *BEAUTIFULLY*, THOUGH, DIDN'T HE?

THAT *WHOLE* THING OUTSIDE MISS HERNANDEZ'S *APARTMENT*, THE *VIDEO CAMERA*, TALK ABOUT GIVING *YOU* A *MOTIVE*.

I HAVE TO *SAY*, RENEE, WHEN YOU GIVE A *BEAT-DOWN*, YOU DON'T *MESS* AROUND.

YOU WERE *WATCHING*?

LONG ENOUGH TO BE *SURE* EVERYTHING WENT THE WAY I WANTED. SOON AS YOU WENT AFTER LIPARI, I WENT TO *HIS* PLACE.

WITH MY *BACKUP.*

RIGHT. YOU WERE HAVING *COFFEE* WITH MISS HERNANDEZ, I WAS *CRACKING* INTO YOUR *GUN SAFE.*

SO WHEN LIPARI GOT BACK TO HIS *APARTMENT*, I WAS THERE. GUNNED HIM DOWN LIKE THE *RAPIST BASTARD* HE WAS.

DROPPING THE *BACKUP* AT THE *SCENE* WAS A MISTAKE. I THOUGHT IT WOULD *READ* AS *OUT* OF *CONTROL*, THAT YOU KILLED LIPARI IN A *RAGE*.

IN RETROSPECT, I SHOULD HAVE PUT IT *BACK* IN YOUR *SAFE* WHEN I PLANTED THE *SMACK*.

ANY *OTHER* QUESTIONS?

WHY'D YOU *SPRING* ME?

AH...YEAH, THAT *WASN'T* MY INITIAL PLAN. BUT AS SOON AS I REALIZED *WAYNE* HAD AN INTEREST, I KNEW YOU'D BE OUT ON *BAIL* BEFORE NIGHTFALL.

IF THAT *HAPPENED*, IT WAS JUST A MATTER OF *TIME* BEFORE THE *CASE* AGAINST YOU *COLLAPSED*.

I HAD TO *NAIL* THE *COFFIN* CLOSED ON YOU.

NOW YOU'RE A *FUGITIVE* ON TOP OF *EVERYTHING* ELSE.

KILLED THE *GUARDS*, TOO?

OF COURSE.

NO, FORGET IT.

I *WON'T* DO THIS, HARVEY. I WON'T *PLAY* AT THIS *ANYMORE!*

SIT *DOWN*, RENEE.

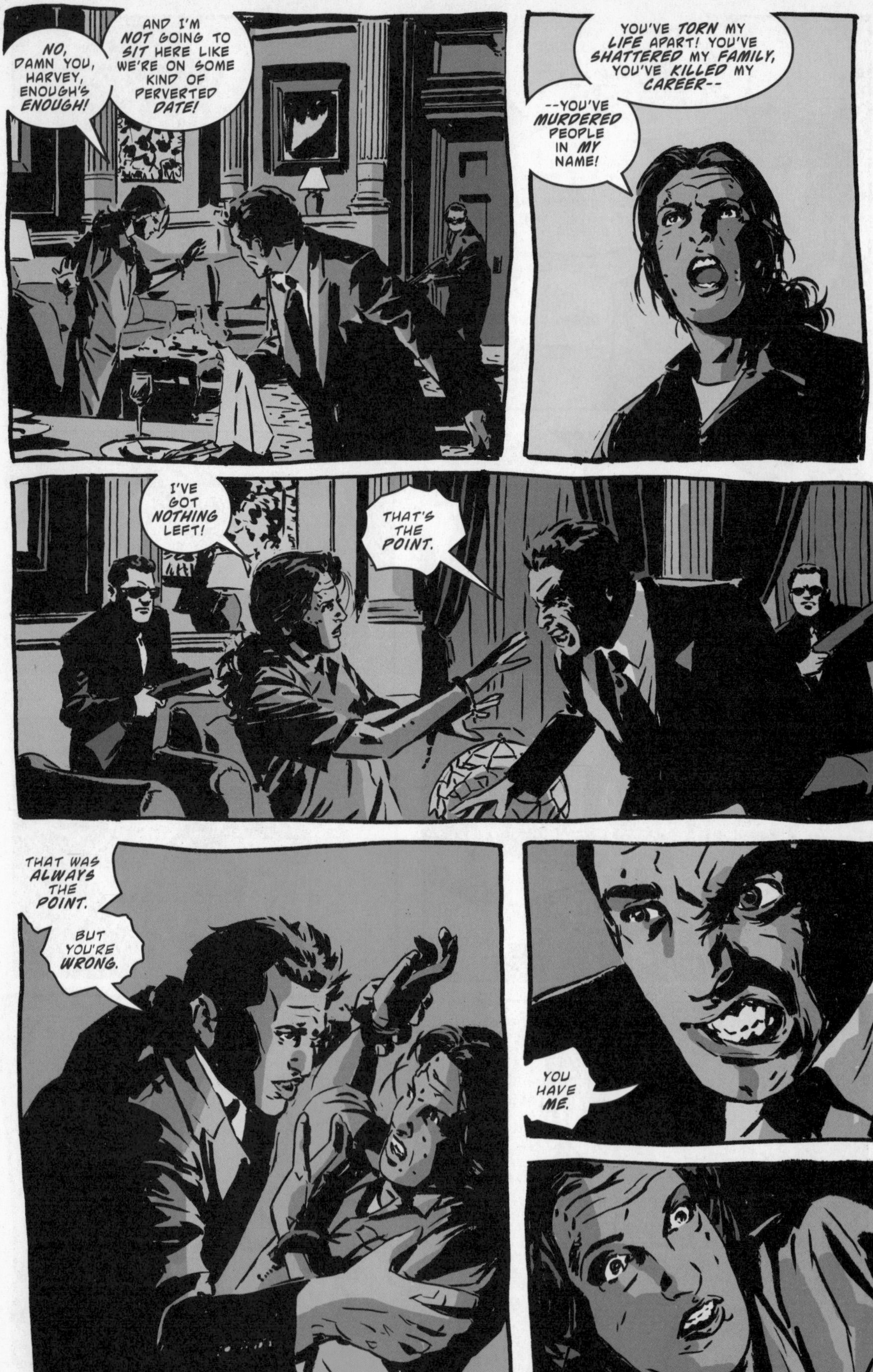
NO, DAMN YOU, HARVEY, ENOUGH'S ENOUGH!
AND I'M NOT GOING TO SIT HERE LIKE WE'RE ON SOME KIND OF PERVERTED DATE!
YOU'VE TORN MY LIFE APART! YOU'VE SHATTERED MY FAMILY, YOU'VE KILLED MY CAREER--
--YOU'VE MURDERED PEOPLE IN MY NAME!
I'VE GOT NOTHING LEFT!
THAT'S THE POINT.
THAT WAS ALWAYS THE POINT.
BUT YOU'RE WRONG.
YOU HAVE ME.

GET OUT.

LEAVE US ALONE.

THIS CONVERSATION ISN'T FOR *THEM*.

DON'T YOU *SEE* IT? YOU'VE BEEN LIVING *TWO LIVES*, AND I'VE *BROKEN DOWN* THE *WALL* BETWEEN THEM.

I'VE *SAVED* YOU.

WE'RE THE *SAME*, RENEE.

AND WE SHOULD BE TOGETH- ER--

--DON'T--

--RUN RENEE THERE'S *NOWHERE* TO RUN--

--IT'S JUST US, NOW--

--YOU AND ME--

--THE WAY WE BOTH KNOW IT SHOULD BE.

WE'RE UNDERGROUND.

YEAH, THIS PLACE GOT PAVED OVER AFTER THE EARTHQUAKE.

FIXED IT UP PRETTY GOOD THOUGH, DIDN'T I?

IT'S OURS, OUR PLACE.

FOR YOU AND ME. WE CAN BE TOGETHER HERE.

YOU'RE THE ONLY PERSON WHO NEVER TREATED ME WITH PITY.

YOU'VE BEEN KIND TO ME. YOU VISITED ME AT ARKHAM.

IT'S OBVIOUS HOW I FEEL ABOUT YOU, RENEE.

AND I THOUGHT THAT, PERHAPS, YOU FELT THE SAME.

THAT YOU LOVED ME, TOO.

HARVEY, *YOU* OUTED ME!

I'M *GAY!* I'M A *DYKE,* A *LESBIAN,* I LIKE *GIRLS!*

DIDN'T YOU LOOK AT THE *PICTURE* BEFORE YOU STARTED SENDING IT AROUND?

YEAH, I *KNOW* ALL THAT.

RENEE, YOU HAVE *NOTHING* TO GO *BACK* TO. I MADE *CERTAIN* OF THAT. YOU'RE STAYING WITH *ME,* NOW.

AND I CAN MAKE YOU *WHOLE.*

NO.

I *DON'T* SEE WHAT *THAT* HAS TO DO WITH *US.*

I *DON'T* LOVE YOU. I'M *NEVER* GOING *TO* LOVE YOU.

AND IF YOU'VE *MISINTERPRETED* THE *KINDNESS* I'VE SHOWN YOU, I AM TRULY SORRY.

BUT YOU WILL *NEVER* GET WHAT YOU *WANT* FROM ME, HARVEY. NOT WILLINGLY, NOT *EVER...*

...AND YOU HAVE TO KNOW THAT I WILL DO *EVERYTHING* I CAN DO TO *ESCAPE* YOU.

NO, *WRONG* ANSWER--

HARVEY--

--SHUT UP, JUST SHUT UP--

--IT'S *HER,* ISN'T IT, THAT *BITCH* CHEF--

--NO HARVEY, SHE HAS *NOTHING* TO DO WITH THIS, THIS IS ABOUT *US*--

LIAR!

LIED TO US!

MISSED ONE, IS *THAT* IT?

AND IF *SHE'S* GONE, THEN WHAT, DETECTIVE? IF I TAKE *HER* FROM YOU, *TOO?* THEN WHAT?

HARVEY, CALM--

HARVEY'S NOT HERE RIGHT NOW!

KILL HER I SHOULD HAVE JUST KILLED HER--

--AND THEN YOU'LL HAVE NOTHING?

--SHOULD I KILL HER, DETECTIVE LIAR SHOULD I TAKE *THAT* FROM YOU *TOO*--

...STOP IT...

152

OH, IT'LL STOP. YES, IT'LL STOP.

ONE WAY OR ANOTHER.

WELL, THEN

LOOKS LIKE I'VE GOT TO *RUN AN ERRAND.*

SHOULDN'T TAKE *TOO* LONG. THE *DOUBLES* WILL LOOK AFTER YOU UNTIL I GET BACK.

TOM! RAY!

WHERE THE HELL ARE THEY?

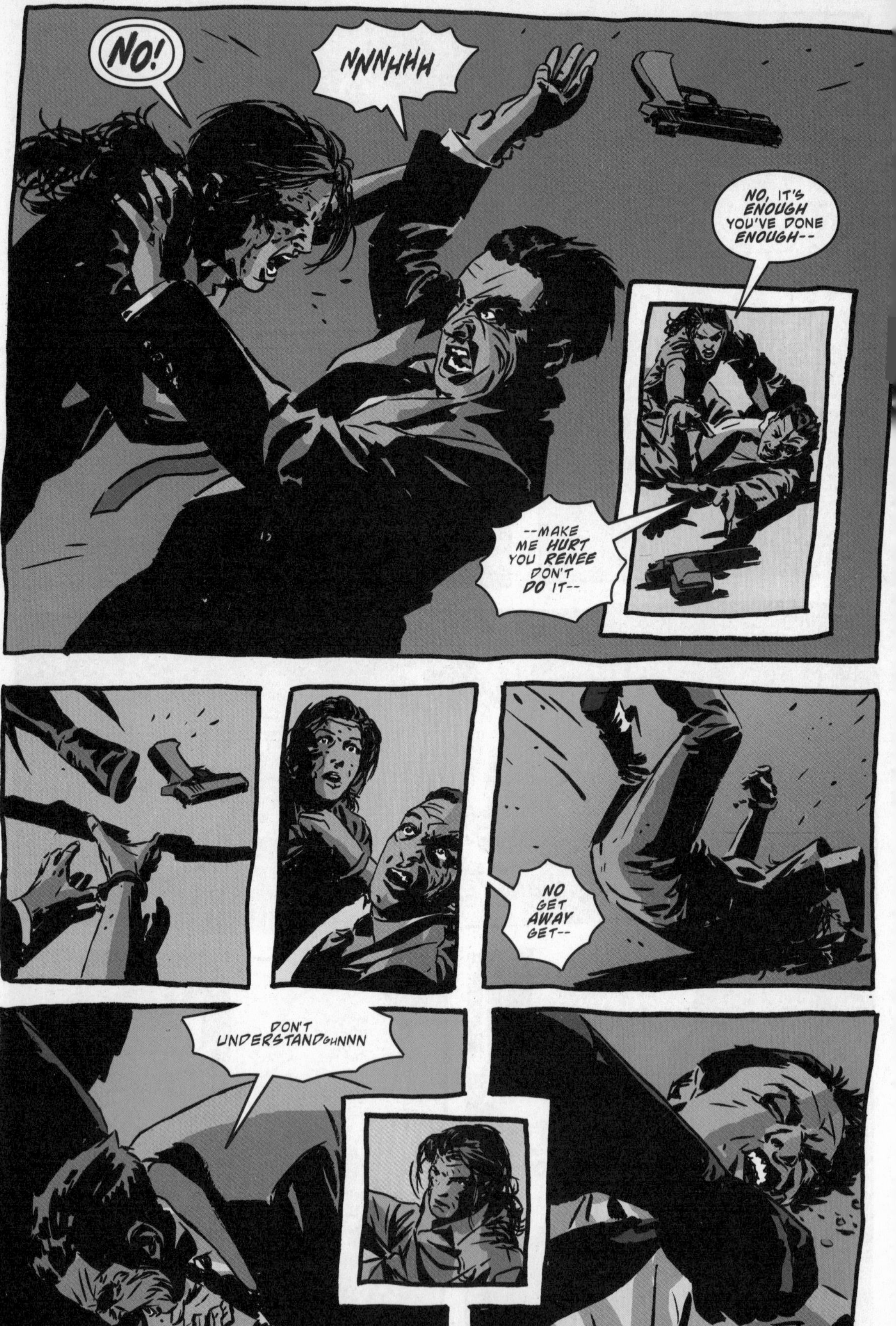
NO!
NNNHHH
NO, IT'S ENOUGH YOU'VE DONE ENOUGH--
--MAKE ME HURT YOU RENEE DON'T DO IT--
NO GET AWAY GET--
DON'T UNDERSTANDGHNNN

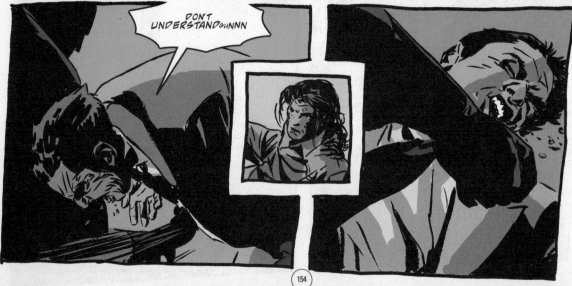

ALLEN AND Q.R.T. ARE *THREE* MINUTES BEHIND ME, DETECTIVE...

...TELL THEM THERE ARE *FOUR* MORE CUFFED IN THE *OTHER* ROOM.

I TOOK *CARE* OF IT.

YOU *WHAT?*

YOU TOOK *CARE* OF THIS? SO HE CAN *BREAK* OUT IN ANOTHER YEAR OR TWO, PUT ME THROUGH THIS *AGAIN?*

THAT'S HOW YOU TOOK CARE OF THIS?

YOU WERE *FIGHTING* FOR THE GUN.

EITHER *HE* WOULD HAVE KILLED *YOU,* OR *YOU* WOULD HAVE KILLED *HIM.*

NEITHER OPTION WAS ACCEPTABLE.

YOU'RE WELCOME.

155

HOW'S THE SWELLING?

YOU TELL ME.

UGLY.

THANKS.

THE "W" IS BUSTED. I THOUGHT THE M.C.U. HAD GOOD EQUIPMENT.

THEN DON'T USE THE "W", ROOKIE.

YOU HAVE ANOTHER WAY TO SPELL "TWO-FACE?"

TRY TWO "O"S.

BATMAN LEAD YOU TO ME?

YEAH. WENT JUST SLOW ENOUGH SO MacDONALD AND I COULD KEEP UP.

APPARENTLY THE BATMAN DOES A MEAN IMPRESSION OF DETECTIVE CROWE.

HE PROBABLY DOES A MEAN IMPRESSION OF ALL OF US.

NOT ME. I'M STILL THE ROOKIE.

EVEN YOU, ROOKIE.

EXCUSE ME.

TELL HER.

IN LIGHT OF INSPECTOR CONWAY'S *CONFESSION* AND THE EVIDENCE COLLECTED WHEN TWO-FACE WAS APPREHENDED, THE D.A.'S OFFICE IS *DIMISSING* ALL CHARGES.

AND *EXTENDING* APOLOGIES.

WHERE IS *HE*?

TWO-FACE IS IN *SECURE* HOLDING AT ARKHAM. HE'LL BE *CHARGED* IN THE MORNING.

LET'S HOPE.

LET'S HOPE *THIS* TIME THEY THROW *AWAY* THE *KEY*.

INSPECTOR ESPERANZA.

CONWAY... HE WAS A *GOOD* COP ONCE, YOU KNOW. TWO-FACE HAS HIS *NUMBER*, THAT'S ALL.

SURE.

OKAY, LET'S TALK ABOUT *YOU*.

I'M READY TO *WORK*.

LIKE *HELL* YOU ARE.

YOU'VE GOT *SIX WEEKS* SAVED UP. YOU'RE GONNA TAKE *FOUR* OF THEM. MacDONALD WILL PARTNER WITH ALLEN UNTIL YOU GET BACK.

AND *IF* I SEE YOU IN *MY* SQUADROOM BEFORE FOUR WEEKS ARE *UP*, DETECTIVE, YOU'LL BE RIDING A *DESK* FOR THE REST OF YOUR CAREER.

I'M GOING TO *SAY* THIS TO YOU AGAIN, RENEE.

WHAT YOU DO NEXT, YOU GET TO LIVE WITH FOR THE *REST* OF YOUR *LIFE*.

YES, MA'AM.

I'LL COME UP *WITH* YOU IF YOU WANT.

NO... PROBABLY *NOT* A GOOD IDEA.

MY *PARENTS* ARE GOING TO FEEL *ATTACKED* AS IT IS...

...HAVING MY *LOVER* WITH ME WILL JUST MAKE THAT *WORSE*.

YOU'VE *NEVER* CALLED ME THAT *BEFORE*.

I *LIKE* IT. IT SOUNDS *GOOD* WHEN YOU SAY IT.

I *KNOW*.

WISH ME LUCK.

YOU'RE THEIR *DAUGHTER,* RENEE. *THAT HASN'T CHANGED.*

I KNOW...

THIS MIGHT *TAKE A WHILE.*

I'LL BE HERE.

RENEE?
HOW'D IT GO?

PRETTY MUCH *EXACTLY* THE WAY I *THOUGHT* IT *WOULD*...

MY *MOTHER* TOLD ME I WAS GOING TO *BURN* IN HELL, AND THAT HER *DAUGHTER* WAS *DEAD* TO HER, NOW...

...SO I *GUESS* WE WERE *WRONG* ABOUT THAT PART, HUH?

MY *FATHER* WOULDN'T *SAY* ANYTHING.

RENEE...

THEY TOLD ME *NOT* TO COME BACK, DEE.

THEY TOLD ME NOT TO *EVER* COME BACK,

...OH GOD...

SHHH, IT'S OKAY, RENEE...

...IT'S OKAY, I'VE GOT YOU...

...OH GOD...

...I'VE GOT YOU...

END

BATMAN CHRONICLES #16 · ART BY JASON PEARSON

DETECTIVE COMICS #747 · ART BY DAVE JOHNSON

GOTHAM CENTRAL #6 · ART BY MICHAEL LARK

GOTHAM CENTRAL #7 · ART BY MICHAEL LARK

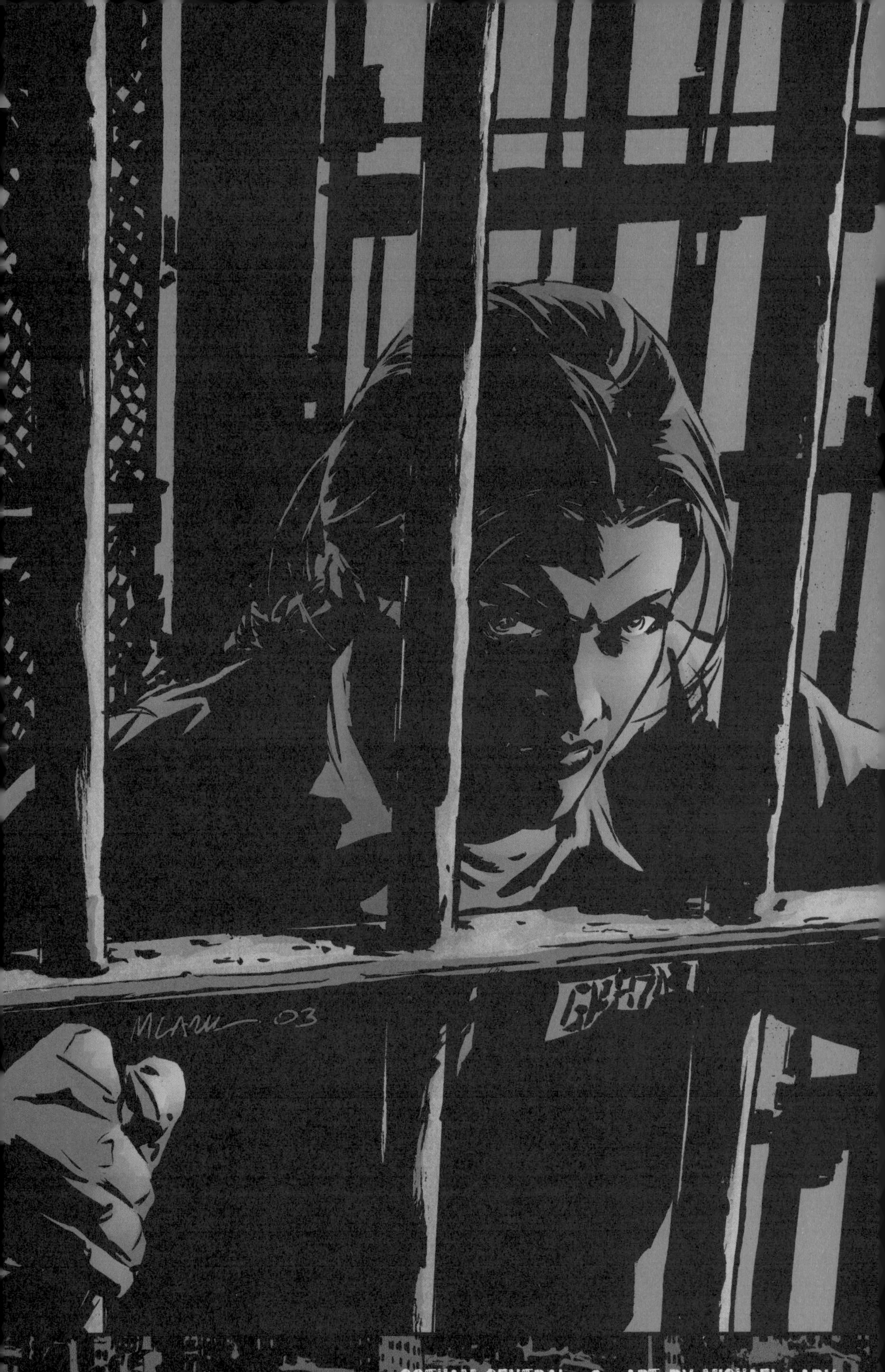

GOTHAM CENTRAL #8 • ART BY MICHAEL LARK

GOTHAM CENTRAL #9 • ART BY MICHAEL LARK

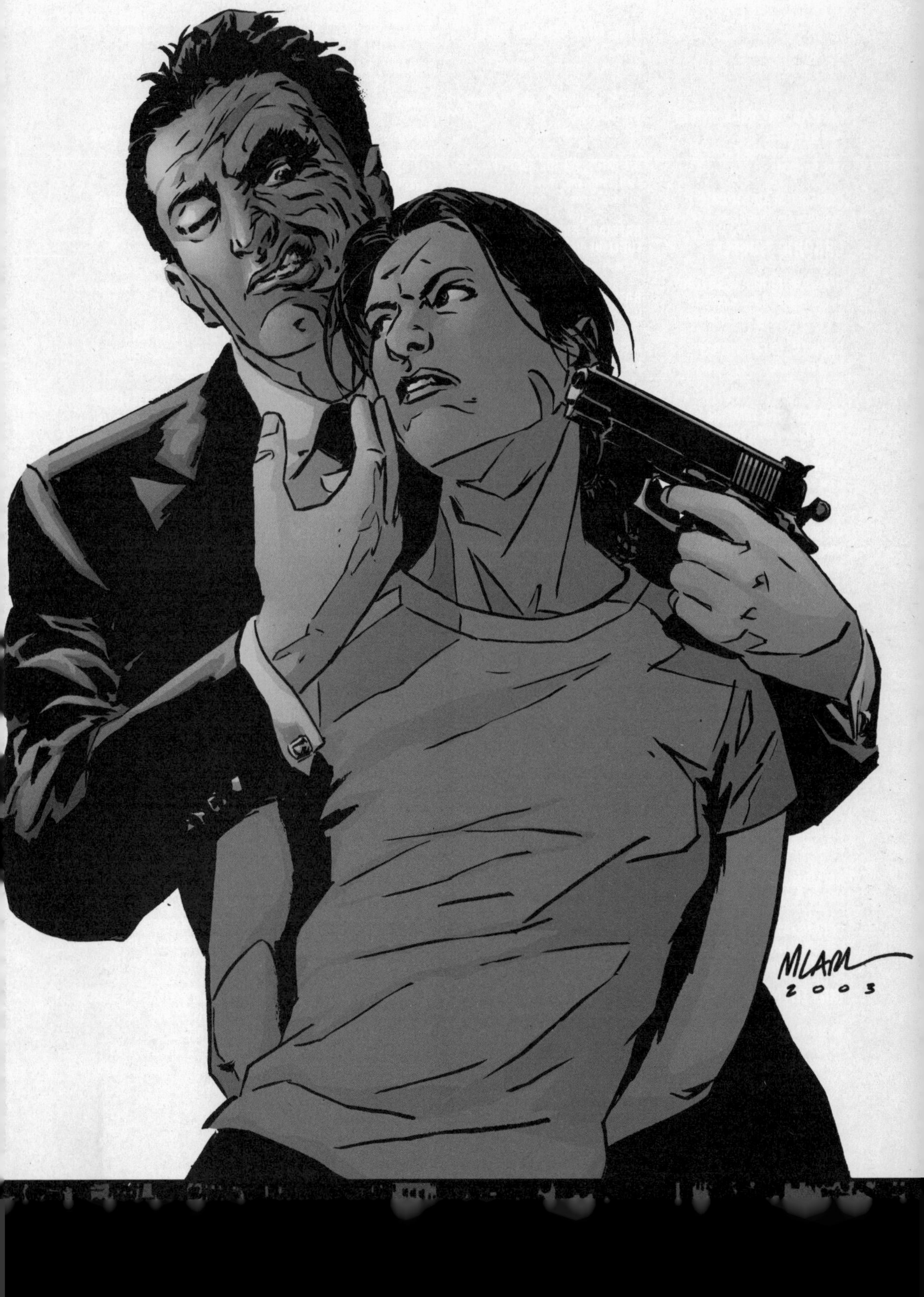

THE QUEST FOR JUSTI... ...E BOOKS FROM DC:

FOR READERS OF ALL AGES

THE BATMAN ADVENTURES
K. Puckett/T. Templeton/
R. Burchett/various

BATMAN BEYOND
Hilary Bader/Rick Burchett/
various

BATMAN: THE DARK KNIGHT ADVENTURES
Kelley Puckett/Mike Parobeck/
Rick Burchett

BATMAN: WAR ON CRIME
Paul Dini/Alex Ross

GRAPHIC NOVELS

BATMAN: ARKHAM ASYLUM
Suggested for mature readers
Grant Morrison/Dave McKean

BATMAN: BLOODSTORM
Doug Moench/Kelley Jones/
John Beatty

BATMAN: THE CHALICE
Chuck Dixon/John Van Fleet

BATMAN: CRIMSON MIST
Doug Moench/Kelley Jones/
John Beatty

BATMAN/DRACULA: RED RAIN
Doug Moench/Kelley Jones/
Malcolm Jones III

BATMAN: FORTUNATE SON
Gerard Jones/Gene Ha

BATMAN: HARVEST BREED
George Pratt

BATMAN: THE KILLING JOKE
Suggested for mature readers
Alan Moore/Brian Bolland/
John Higgins

BATMAN: NIGHT CRIES
Archie Goodwin/Scott Hampton

BATMAN: NINE LIVES
Dean Motter/Michael Lark

BATMAN: SON OF THE DEMON
Mike Barr/Jerry Bingham

**CATWOMAN:
SELINA'S BIG SCORE**
Darwyn Cooke

COLLECTIONS

BATMAN: A DEATH IN THE FAMILY
Jim Starlin/Jim Aparo/
Mike DeCarlo

BATMAN: A LONELY PLACE OF DYING
Marv Wolfman/George Pérez/
various

BATMAN BLACK AND WHITE Vols. 1 & 2
Various writers and artists

BATMAN: BRUCE WAYNE — MURDERER?
Various writers and artists

BATMAN: BRUCE WAYNE — FUGITIVE Vol. 1
Various writers and artists

BATMAN: EVOLUTION
Rucka/Martinbrough/Mitchell/
various

BATMAN: GOTHIC
Grant Morrison/Klaus Janson

BATMAN: HAUNTED KNIGHT
Jeph Loeb/Tim Sale

BATMAN/HUNTRESS: CRY FOR BLOOD
Rucka/Burchett/T. Beatty

**BATMAN IN THE FIFTIES
BATMAN IN THE SIXTIES
BATMAN IN THE SEVENTIES**
Various writers and artists

**THE KNIGHTFALL Trilogy
BATMAN: KNIGHTFALL Part 1:
Broken Bat
BATMAN: KNIGHTFALL Part 2:
Who Rules the Night**

BATMAN: KNIGHTFALL Part 3: KnightsEnd
Various writers and artists

BATMAN: THE LONG HALLOWEEN
Jeph Loeb/Tim Sale

BATMAN: NO MAN'S LAND Vols. 1 - 5
Various writers and artists

BATMAN: OFFICER DOWN
Various writers and artists

BATMAN: PRODIGAL

BATGIRL: SILENT RUNNING
Puckett/Peterson/D. Scott/
Campanella

BIRDS OF PREY
Various writers and artists

BIRDS OF PREY: OLD FRIENDS, NEW ENEMIES
Dixon/Land/Geraci/various

CATWOMAN: THE DARK END OF THE STREET
Brubaker/Cooke/Allred

THE GREATEST BATMAN STORIES EVER TOLD Vol. 1
Various writers and artists

THE GREATEST JOKER STORIES EVER TOLD
Various writers and artists

NIGHTWING: A KNIGHT IN BLÜDHAVEN
Dixon/McDaniel/Story

NIGHTWING: ROUGH JUSTICE
Dixon/McDaniel/Story

NIGHTWING: LOVE AND BULLETS
Dixon/McDaniel/Story

NIGHTWING: A DARKER SHADE OF JUSTICE
Dixon/McDaniel/Story

NIGHTWING: THE HUNT FOR ORACLE
Dixon/Land/Guice/Zircher/various

ROBIN: FLYING SOLO
Dixon/Grummett/P. Jimenez/
various

ROBIN: YEAR ONE
Dixon/S. Beatty/Pulido/
Martin/Campanella

ARCHIVE EDITIONS

BATMAN ARCHIVES Vol. 1
(DETECTIVE COMICS 27-50)
BATMAN ARCHIVES Vol. 2
(DETECTIVE COMICS 51-70)
BATMAN ARCHIVES Vol. 3
(DETECTIVE COMICS 71-86)
BATMAN ARCHIVES Vol. 4
(DETECTIVE COMICS 87-102)
BATMAN ARCHIVES Vol. 5
(DETECTIVE COMICS 103-119)
All by B. Kane/B. Finger/D. Sprang/
various

BATMAN: THE DARK KNIGHT ARCHIVES Vol. 1
(BATMAN 1-4)
BATMAN: THE DARK KNIGHT ARCHIVES Vol. 2
(BATMAN 5-8)
BATMAN: THE DARK KNIGHT ARCHIVES Vol. 3
(BATMAN 9-12)
All by Bob Kane/Bill Finger/various

BATMAN: THE DYNAMIC DUO ARCHIVES Vol. 1
(BATMAN 164-167,
DETECTIVE COMICS 327-333)
B. Kane/Giella/Finger/Broome/
Fox/various

WORLD'S FINEST COMICS ARCHIVES Vol. 1
(SUPERMAN 76,
WORLD'S FINEST 71-85)
B. Finger/E. Hamilton/C. Swan/
Sprang/various

**TO FIND MORE COLLECTED EDITIONS AND MONTHLY COMIC BOOKS FROM DC COMICS,
CALL 1-888-COMIC BOOK FOR THE NEAREST COMICS SHOP OR GO TO YOUR LOCAL BOOK STORE.**

Visit us at www.dccomics.com

BM0012